MW00581789

LIFE IS A DANCE
IF YOU TAKE THE STEPS

How to "Work" the 12 Steps of Alcoholics Anonymous

WRITTEN BY
CYNTHIA EMMETS

Copyright © 2005 by Cynthia Emmets

All rights reserved. No part of this book shall be reproduced or transmitted in any form or by any means, electronic, mechanical, magnetic, photographic including photocopying, recording or by any information storage and retrieval system, without prior written permission of the publisher. No patent liability is assumed with respect to the use of the information contained herein. Although every precaution has been taken in the preparation of this book, the publisher and author assume no responsibility for errors or omissions. Neither is any liability assumed for damages resulting from the use of the information contained herein.

ISBN 0-7414-2383-9

Published by:

INFINITY
PUBLISHING.COM

1094 New De Haven Street, Suite 100
West Conshohocken, PA 19428-2713
Info@buybooksontheweb.com
www.buybooksontheweb.com
Toll-free (877) BUY BOOK
Local Phone (610) 941-9999
Fax (610) 941-9959

Printed in the United States of America

Printed on Recycled Paper

Published February 2005

DISCLAIMER

The Twelve Steps are reprinted with permission of Alcoholics Anonymous World Services, Inc. (A.A.W.S.) Permission to reprint the Twelve Steps does not mean that A.A.W.S. has reviewed or approved the contents of this publication, or that A.A.W.S. necessarily agrees with the views expressed herein. A.A. is a program of recovery from alcoholism <u>only</u> - use of the Twelve Steps in connection with programs and activities which are patterned after A.A., but which address other problems, or in any other non-A.A. context, does not imply otherwise.

TABLE OF CONTENTS

Twelve Steps of Alcoholics Anonymous

1. We admitted we were powerless over alcohol -- that our lives had become unmanageable.

2. Came to believe that a Power greater than ourselves could restore us to sanity.

3. Made a decision to turn our will and our lives over to the care of God as we understood Him.

4. Made a searching and fearless moral inventory of ourselves.

5. Admitted to God, to ourselves, and to another human being the exact nature of our wrongs.

6. Were entirely ready to have God remove all these defects of character.

7. Humbly asked Him to remove our shortcomings.

8. Made a list of all people we had harmed and became willing to make amends to them all.

9. Made direct amends to such people, wherever possible, except when to do so would injure them or others.

10. Continued to take personal inventory and when we were wrong, promptly admitted it.

11. Sought through prayer and meditation to improve our conscious contact with God, as we understood Him, praying only for knowledge of His will for us and the power to carry that out.

12. Having had a spiritual awakening as the result of these steps, we tried to carry this message to alcoholics, and to practice these principles in all our affairs.

WHAT IT USED TO BE LIKE, WHAT HAPPENED, AND WHAT IT'S LIKE NOW

In September of 1984, the Twelve Steps of Alcoholics Anonymous relieved me of the obsession to compulsively overeat, drink and use drugs. But once those substances were removed, the issues hiding behind them slowly emerged like a tiger waiting for the right moment to pounce on its prey. I found freedom from substances only the **beginning** of my journey, not the end of it. I was facing another obsession even more difficult to overcome: the desire to be in a loving relationship and get married. With no healthy relationship in sight and my dating history less than stellar, it seemed I was destined to be alone forever. Until I discovered the Twelve Steps held the solution to this problem too.

I was attracted to the "bad boys". You know, the ones with leather jackets, goatees and a few well-placed tats. The ones who were emotionally and usually physically unavailable. The ones I had to chase, who never called, never asked a single question about my life but told me more about theirs than I ever needed to know. Musicians, (with or without a job), actors, (with or without a job), construction workers (with or without a job), surfers (usually without a job), or those who lived hundreds of miles away (with or without a job). Guys who were sure to criticize me for my body, my friends, anything they could find that would make them feel better about themselves. Guys who were sure to leave me and never wanted to make a commitment. Those were just my type.

I could spot one across a crowded room and love (or was that lust?) was in the air. Adrenaline made my heart pump faster than cocaine. My breath came as irregularly as if I were choking to death. I couldn't understand why, after a few months of dating, we always crashed and burned. I kept thinking I'd found my knight in shining armor but he always turned out to be my <u>nightmare</u> in shining armor.

I read dozens of self-help books on how to find the man of my dreams and have a healthy relationship. They explained actions I should be doing differently; gave me "rules" on what to do to hook a man; provided psychological analyses of the differences between men and women and how to speak to them so they'd understand. I listened to cassettes on codependency and counterdependency. I watched talk shows whenever the subject was attracting the man of your dreams, but was frustrated because the thirty-second sound bytes gave me no directions on what to do. I went into therapy and delved into my past, but got no suggestions for the present. I had all this self-knowledge and understanding about relationships, as well as a list of actions I'd taken to find "Mr. Right", but after three years, I was still single and as clueless as before.

Without being consciously aware of what I was doing, I began to blame men for my situation. Not a man, but men as a species. It became all their fault. It must be my business savvy, success and independence that intimidated them. They just wanted a woman they would have to take care of to build their egos. Men didn't really believe women were equal; they were only being politically correct. Was I caught in the hell of some multi-generational gap between women's liberation and the 50's? Or were all the good ones already taken? Maybe my "picker" was chronically broken, making me chose only emotionally unavailable men.

Then it was my Higher Power's turn to take the blame. I was sick of hearing if I'd only find God's love inside me I would be fulfilled. I listened to friends' well-meaning words, but said to myself, "They don't understand. I do have a great relationship with God. I also want someone to hold me at night and a partner to live my life with." I was enraged that God wasn't following my plan and my timeline. He just wasn't cooperating. I had almost run out of solutions. Almost.

Then I met Rodney. This time, I was more certain than ever that I found HIM. You know - the guy who gives you the shakes when you hear his voice on the phone, who sends bolts of electricity in your body the minute he holds your hand. The one whose every joke is hilarious, whose every word you hang on. That kind of HIM. This time I knew I was really in love. I didn't realize I had just met the man who would show me how much I still had to learn about what love is.

It was a radiant summer Sunday afternoon. I attended a blues festival in a romantic and intimate outdoor amphitheater in the middle of beautiful Topanga Canyon, California. Surrounding the amphitheater were trees, flowers and bushes, all green and lush from the recent rains, glistening in the brilliant Los Angeles sunshine.

Rod was seated on the blanket directly in front of me with a pretty woman whom I assumed to be his date. For this reason, I barely paid any attention to him throughout most of the daylong show. However, as often happens at events where your neighbor is less than six inches away from you for five straight hours, the woman and I struck up a conversation. It turned out she was Rod's cousin. She introduced me to Rod and made it very clear that Rod was unattached and I should be friendlier to him for the rest of the concert. After finding out that Rod was fair game (that was how I thought of men at that time) I took my first good look at him and thought, "He could be real trouble." I was right.

Rod had wavy reddish-brown hair that he unconsciously tossed to the side when he laughed. And he laughed often, with an infectious, boyish giggle. His horned-rimmed glasses made him a fascinating contradiction between a studious university professor and a carefree child. He had a reddish Van Dyke that framed his chin and begged to be stroked. His body was that of a swimmer: large barrel chest, broad shoulders, small waist and tight buns. (OK, so I appreciate nice buns).

Our initial conversations were limited, but the intense attraction we had for each other seemed to overshadow every word. As a songwriter, I was thrilled to meet someone who shared my love of music, especially blues. And he was a great dancer! We danced together to every song for the rest of the show. The last song was a slow, sexy number. With Rod behind me, his arms around my waist, we swayed in unison, hip to hip, my back to his chest. After the song was over, he turned me around and gave me a long, slow, wet kiss that made my toes tingle. I was completely hooked. He asked if he could see me again, and I said, "Sure!" (I now know that that one word was my entrance fee into the most excruciating pain I had yet to feel, as well as the blissful happiness I now have.)

He said, "OK. I'll give you my phone number."

I cut him off immediately. "I won't call you. I don't call men." I was proud of myself, starting off this potential relationship on the right foot.

He then asked me for my phone number and I handed him my songwriter card with my home number on it. In exchange, he tore off a piece of paper and wrote, **"Rodney, N'er Do Well"** with his phone number. Right there, Rod was practically erecting a billboard of who he was. But denial runs deep and I proceeded full speed ahead, forgetting all my past hurts and warning signs. I was blind. I was smitten. The physical attraction had taken over and my hormones ruled.

Rod called me the following Tuesday. It was all I could do to hide how excited I was to hear from him. We went out several nights later and thus began the most torrid romance I had ever had. We spoke on the phone for hours each night, talking about politics, our interests, our day and sex. We walked on the beach, drank coffee in sidewalk cafes, went to hear live blues and bluegrass music, went dancing - everything I loved to do.

After five months of serious dating, some invisible internal alarm clock went off in me. There was a voice that kept repeating, "Time to move the relationship to the next level. You've got to get married now that you've turned 40, Cynthia!"

Rodney, however, didn't agree. He liked the relationship just the way it was. This time, I decided to take control rather than waste any more precious time. "Maybe that's the solution", I thought. "Yes," I convinced myself, "this will stop the insanity of my dating unavailable men. I'll send a message to the Universe that I won't stand for it anymore."

I called Rod and said it was over. He was truly surprised. We both cried on the phone and said that we loved each other. I hung up, then threw up.

There are moments in your life when you look back and realize the road you'd been traveling on suddenly took a giant left turn. The moment where everything you used to be suddenly changes. **That** moment was when I hung up the phone after saying good-bye to Rod for the last time. In 20/20 hindsight, I see it was one of the major turning points in my life. I became so depressed I contemplated suicide. I was grieving the loss of the fantasy of who I thought Rod was, what we could have become, the wedding which never was, complete with white dress, multi-tiered cake and bridesmaids. I kept reliving the fun we'd had and was convinced I'd just thrown away the man of my dreams.

I hit a bottom like never before. I wasn't prepared for what happened next. For the first time in seven years of not drinking, I wanted to die. Not drink -- **DIE.** There's nothing like hitting bottom to force one into action, especially if your life depends upon it! I was finally out of solutions. It dawned on me that neither God, circumstances, nor the men I dated were to blame - *I* was.

Now being the cause of my problems was bad news and good news. Bad news because I could no longer play the victim by pointing the finger at anyone or anything else. Good news because, if I'm the problem, I could also be the solution.

I knew the Steps had removed my food, alcohol and drug addictions. Could they work for other things too? How could they be used as a solution to problems with LIVING? I knew how to ***read*** the Steps, ***understand*** the Steps, but even after seven years, I had no clue on what it meant to "***work***" the Steps on anything other than my substance abuse. This workbook was born out of my own desperate attempt to understand how to "***work*** the Steps" on my wanting a healthy relationship and marriage. I was grasping desperately at a peace I knew only the Steps and my Higher Power could give me.

Life Is A Dance If You Take the Steps began simply by my writing a letter to God every day. In these letters, I would write about each Step and how to apply it to my obsession of wanting a relationship. Since I'm a former teacher, I have years of experience creating workbook exercises to simplify difficult concepts and theories, breaking them down into smaller pieces for students to digest.

Considering myself a student in the classroom of love, I developed a series of workbook exercises that analyze my failed relationships, eased past hurts, and showed me what I could and could not change about relationships. I couldn't change other people, but the good news was that I **could** change me. I stopped pointing the finger at men and at God and focused on the three fingers pointing back at me. I gave up the myth that romance is love and instead discovered true love requires lots of work on my part.

I'd like to be able to tell you that creating and then working the exercises in this workbook completely relieved me of the obsession to have a relationship and get married without my having to go through more pain in the process. Being rigorously honest, I went through the experience of a brief, yet unhappy marriage before my heart fully embraced the truth: love is not something one needs to get from outside. It's inside each of us.

"No duh," you say. OK. Seems so obvious, but I continued to force my control to try to get what I thought I wanted. The pain was caused by the difficulty in surrendering to God's timing and accepting that everything was happening just as it was supposed to. I couldn't believe God was handling everything in His perfect time.

"So what's the point of doing the workbook exercises if you still had to go through the heartache of an unhappy marriage?" you probably want to ask me.

God doesn't waste any experiences. I learned a very valuable lesson and had a spiritual awakening thanks to that marriage that I pass along in this workbook: the results of a relationship are in God's Hands, not mine.

My marriage pushed me to the point where I was finally unwilling to be something I'm not in order to get or keep a relationship; unwilling to say something I didn't mean just to please a man; unwilling to do things I didn't want to do so I could keep a man. I could stop performing to convince a man I was lovable.

After that unhappy marriage and the spiritual awakening that followed, I decided I was so happy being alone that I didn't have any interest in ever having a relationship again. Once again, God had other plans. On Thanksgiving Day, 1994, I dedicated the day to God and did all the exercises in the workbook on the problems with my marriage. In my Seventh Step, I asked God to help me respect men as friends instead of evaluating them as potential mates. I prayed for relief from my character defenses of making other people, places and things my Higher Power.

The very next day, I received a call from David, a man whom I had met at a wedding three months prior. He had taken my number at the time, but had never called me. He asked me out on a date for that Saturday night. Because I was so happy being alone and didn't want to put the effort into dating, I lied and said I already had plans. He was extremely persistent however. He asked me out for Sunday night and again I made up an excuse and declined. When he said, "What about tonight?" I had run out of excuses, and I heard myself saying okay.

I had always been taught to believe that if I looked pretty enough, was quiet and didn't ask for anything, got good grades, was funny, or became whatever someone else wanted, I'd get what I wanted, including a relationship. After some of the lessons like Rodney, my ex-husband and others, I learned the true meaning of powerlessness and letting go. I came to believe in my heart what people had been telling me for so long: ***if a relationship is meant to be, it will be,***

regardless of what I do or don't do. There was nothing wrong with me; if the relationship wasn't working, it wasn't meant to work. Rejection was my Higher Power protection.

He had something better in mind for me if I'd just let go. I made a vow to never again change who I was to please someone else, to hide my feelings, to not express what was bothering me, or to sweep problems under the rug to avoid confrontation. Though that was a really hard concept to internalize, it has been the saving grace in all my relationships: work, friends, and especially with David.

When I first starting dating David, I put everything on the table right from the start. He was a bicycle enthusiast who loves to camp, hike and backpack. I told him that I wouldn't be joining him on any backpacking trips or going biking, camping or hiking with him and that my idea of camping is a hotel without a concierge. If he was looking for a woman to share those activities with, he should go find someone else right away. That way, I didn't set up any false expectations.

However, the more deeply I began to care for him, the harder it became to stand my ground. We'd been dating about six months when he told me he was going on vacation with his ex-girlfriend's sister. I was furious because his job afforded him very little vacation time, and that meant we wouldn't be spending it together. The old me would've said, "Okay honey. No problem". I would have wanted to be the "good girlfriend", ignore my feelings, swallow my anger and not create a scene. But I would have seethed inside and given him the silent treatment when he got back.

This time, I spent about a week thinking and praying about it, used the exercises in this book, and knew without a doubt that I could never accept this. I became willing to let go of the relationship if he went on vacation with her and I told him so. I wasn't angry; I just was no longer willing to give myself up. I trusted that if the relationship was meant to be, it would be, regardless of what I did or did not do.

Of course, this book has a happy ending, and he didn't go on vacation with her. He and I went to Sedona, Arizona together and had a wonderful time. He got to ride his mountain bike and I got to meditate in some of the holiest spots.

That was 10 years ago and we've been together ever since. He moved in with me 9 years ago. We're truly in love, not in need. And I don't want to get married! I am free of that obsession, thanks to the exercises in my workbook that helped me use the Steps to find a solution to that problem.

By sharing this workbook with hundreds of people, I've watched both men and women use *Life Is A Dance If You Take the Steps* to solve <u>any</u> problem, not just that of wanting a relationship. The Steps are malleable enough to fit any scenario if you "work" them. Additionally, although the exercises can be successful for everyone, male and female, *Life Is A Dance If You Take the Steps* is slanted toward a woman's point of view (the fact that I'm a woman probably has something to do with it!) The issues a woman faces are different than those of a man and, because the literature of Alcoholics Anonymous is written from a man's perspective, a woman sometimes has trouble identifying with its language and concepts. The workbook, on the other hand, provides an interpretation and language of the Steps that is relevant to today's woman and helps explore and heal those issues. There are even examples on how to complete each exercise from my own personal experiences.

Hopefully, thanks to the workbook, you can benefit from, and avoid my painful experiences. Above all, I trust the workbook will help you release your anger from the past, erase your fears of intimacy and abandonment, recognize and let go of society's unrealistic definition of love and remove any blocks you unconsciously place in your own path to having a loving relationship. Like me, after you have found a new you, the man of your dreams may find you!

DEFINING THE SPECIFIC PROBLEM

You're ready to begin. Write down a problem or issue that you are having, which you intend to use the exercises in the workbook to solve. Just a sentence or two will do.

Here's my example:

MY PROBLEM TODAY IS:

Example: I want a relationship and I don't have one.

Write down your specific problem:

MY PROBLEM TODAY IS:

_____

_____

_____

_____

_____

STEP ONE: ADMITTED WE WERE POWERLESS OVER ALCOHOL -- THAT OUR LIVES HAD BECOME UNMANAGEABLE

"We stand ready to do anything which will lift the merciless obsession from us." (Page 24, Twelve Steps and Twelve Traditions of Alcoholics Anonymous)

When I think I'm in charge of my own life and I'm not going to get what I want when I want it, I haven't taken Step One. I know I'm not working this Step when I'm angry because things aren't going my way. Maybe I have a million things on my To-Do list for the day and I'm frustrated because I'm not able to cross them all off. Or I'm supposed to be at a certain place by a certain time and I get stuck in traffic. Or, as you've already read, I tried to manipulate getting a relationship. Step One means I've forgotten that a Power greater than me is taking care of everything. I'm in fear and my immediate reaction is to try to control.

Before I can let go of the fear and controlling behavior, I have to ***admit*** that I need help. First I try to force a square peg solution into a round hole. Then a diamond-shaped peg. Then a triangle-shaped one. Once I have run out of my own ideas for solutions, I end up face down on the floor crying to God. I wish I didn't have to get so desperate before I surrender, but I do, especially if it's something I want really badly. At this point, I have a choice, Step One, or Step Zero. I've heard it said that if you are having trouble working a Step, go back to the one before it. I define Step Zero as "Prayed for the willingness to admit I was powerless"!

If you're ready to take Step One, the exercises below are designed to help you realize you are powerless, even if you haven't yet admitted it. They will help you realize where you're trying to exert your own power trying to make something happen rather than letting it happen. You will also see whether or not your efforts are working. (Remember, ***your best efforts*** have gotten you to be as uncomfortable as you are right now!)

Exercise 1.1: What Am I Powerless Over?

Rewrite this Step, changing the word "alcohol" to whatever you defined as your problem on the previous page. Also change the word "we" to "I." Here's what I wrote:

Example: *Exercise 1.1*:

Admitted I was powerless over <u>wanting a relationship and not having one</u> (the problem I listed as the one I wanted to work the Steps on this time) and my life had become unmanageable.

Now your turn:

_____

_____

_____

_____

_____

Exercise 1.2: What I'm Trying To Have Some Power Over

Oftentimes, when doing Step One, we list the things we admit we **are** powerless over. However, in *Exercise 1.2*, we look at things we are **not** admitting we are powerless over because we're exerting our own will. Battling with the need for control seems to be a major struggle we face after a few years of recover for many of us. Sometimes, we even know **intellectually** we don't have any control over a person, place or thing, but that still doesn't stop us from trying to make things go our way. When we try to control a situation or person, it often gets worse. We re-double our efforts at control. When that doesn't work, we are finally forced to say to ourselves, "I give up! I can't make this work. My life has become unmanageable around trying to force a solution to this problem." At this point we become willing to give up, and ask for help from our Higher Power.

I knew my life was unmanageable around my obsession of wanting a relationship because it was the only thing I thought about and the motivation for almost everything I did. Once I saw what I was trying to control, what I was doing to control it, and how deeply it was hurting me, it was easier to let go and let God.

There are three columns in this exercise. In the first column, list the persons, places and things you are trying to control. In the second column, next to each person, place or thing, write down ways you have tried to control it. In the last column, write down how your attempts to control have hurt you, or have made your life unmanageable. Here is an example, using my problem of wanting a relationship and not having one:

Example: ***Exercise 1.2: So You Think You're Not a Control Freak?***

WHAT I TRY TO CONTROL	WAYS I TRY TO CONTROL	WAYS CONTROLLING MAKES MY LIFE UNMANAGEABLE
Having a relationship	• Go to places where I might find "HIM" • Accept dates with men I don't really want to go out with • Join clubs with male members • Don't accept invitations unless there will be lots of men there	• I get sick and can't go to work because I stay out too late • I don't see a man for who he is, only as a potential mate • I stop doing my favorite hobbies unless they involve men
What a man thinks of me	• Flirt • Wear sexy clothes • Pretend to always be in a good mood around him • Don't get angry even when I have a reason to • Have sex when I don't want to	• I reinforce my low self-esteem by not being who I really am • I accept unacceptable behavior • I'm spending more money on clothes than I have • I'm not setting the boundaries I need to
Getting married	• Blame men for not being who I want them to be • Choose unavailable men • Stay in unhealthy relationships	• Sell myself short • Don't open up to accept all kinds of men • Stay in denial about my own fears of intimacy

Here's your chance to take an honest look at your attempts to control a situation. Remember; be as thorough as you can!

Exercise 1.2: So You Think You're Not a Control Freak?

WHAT I'M TRYING TO CONTROL	WAYS I TRY TO CONTROL	WAYS CONTROLLING MAKES MY LIFE UNMANAGEABLE

STEP TWO: CAME TO BELIEVE THAT A POWER GREATER THAN OURSELVES COULD RESTORE US TO SANITY

"At no time had we asked what God's will was for us; instead, we had been telling Him what it ought to be. No man, we saw, could believe in God and defy Him too. Belief meant reliance, not defiance." (Page 31, Twelve Steps and Twelve Traditions of Alcoholics Anonymous)

Go back and look at what you've written in *Exercise 1.2*. Based on what you see, how could you NOT admit you need some help? If what you've been doing isn't working, let's take a leap of faith to the next level: try believing in a Power greater than yourself. You can call It whatever you like: Higher Power, or Spirit, or Universe, H.P. or God. **Remember that you don't need to think of this Higher Power as a traditional God,** although if you already have One, great! Pick your own – whatever works for you. You need only believe that <u>some</u> Power exists that's greater than you. Those of you who are card-carrying atheists like I was may have trouble with this, but what can you lose by trying it? That was the question I asked myself and the answer for me was <u>nothing</u>! Nevertheless, stick with me on this because you may need to switch Higher Powers to one that's more unconditionally loving.

If you're adamant about holding onto your belief that there's no Power greater than you, let's test that theory. Go down to the ocean and tell the waves to stop rolling. If they stop, please contact me immediately because I'd like to be your agent! If they don't stop rolling, there *<u>IS</u>* a Power greater than you. If you still have your doubts, go back and look again at *Exercise 1.2* to be reminded that what you've been doing isn't working!

Some things are appropriate to recognize as having more power than you: nature, the wind or the Universe. Some people, places and things aren't. Even before I started to believe in the Higher Power I have now (who DOES make the waves roll), I spent a lifetime of unconsciously making men, bosses, authority figures, and other people my higher power by turning my self-esteem over to them. Not a good thing and one I continually struggle with.

Exercise 2.1: Who's Got the Power?

Before we define your Higher Power, let's take a look at what or whom you are currently making your higher power. There are two columns: Column One asks you to list the material things to which you **give** power and in Column Two list those that legitimately **have** more power than you. Hang onto this exercise until you get to Step Four, when Column 1 will be used again.

Exercise 2.1: Who's Got the Power?

Example:

MATERIAL THINGS TO WHICH I GIVE POWER	THINGS WHICH HAVE MORE POWER THAN ME
• Men	• Nature
• Bosses	• God
• Politicians	• The wind
• Money	• The ocean
• Jobs	• The Universe
• Fear	• Love

Exercise 2.1 Who's Got the Power?:

List the things that have more power than you, and those to which you give power:

MATERIAL THINGS TO WHICH I GIVE POWER	THINGS WHICH HAVE MORE POWER THAN ME

Exercise 2.2: Wanted: One Higher Power

Each time I do Step Two, I choose a Power more loving than the One before. My Higher Power, whom I choose to call God, has changed over the years. It started as a traditional deity, evolved into something akin to a Star Trek-kind of Higher Power, and now I believe it's the Universal Love inside each of us. For those of you who are atheists or agnostics, ignore the fact that I use the word God throughout the workbook. Please remember I am referring to my definition of a Higher Power and you will define your own.

In Step Two we begin the process of defining our own Higher Power and understanding how truly insane our behavior has been. In *Exercise 2.1* above, you listed things that **legitimately** have more power than you. Choose one of them to be your Higher Power. This Higher Power will be your Source of strength to help you identify solutions through the Steps. (By the way, I wouldn't recommend choosing another person to be your Higher Power! Remember that he/she is only human and is probably having a hard enough time trying to run his/her own life, let alone be responsible for taking care of yours!)

It's helpful to know a little more about the Higher Power you've chosen. *Exercise 2.2* helps you put your own definition to the Higher Power you want. This exercise is especially healing if you grew up with a punishing and vengeful God that may have made you turn away from a Higher Power altogether. You also can fire the Higher Power you've had and replace It with a new One!

Example: *Exercise 2.2: WANTED -- ONE HIGHER POWER*

Write a Want Ad for your Higher Power, just like the classified ads you see in the newspaper. Mine looked like this:

WANTED: ONE HIGHER POWER

Must be unconditionally loving, have an incredible sense of humor, be patient, comforting, gentle, forgiving, and understanding. On call 24/7. Willing to travel anywhere and everywhere with me all the time. Must be all-powerful and all-knowing.

What do you want from your Higher Power? Write your own Want Ad below:

Exercise 2.2: WANTED -- ONE HIGHER POWER

_____

_____

_____

_____

_____

Go ahead! If you want to, fire your old Higher Power, whoever or whatever It was, and hire this One. Tell your new Higher Power the good news – He (or She or It) has been selected for the position you outlined in your Want Ad. This Higher Power will be on the job until you are ready for a new One.

Exercise 2.3: Up Close and Personal

In *Exercise 2.2*, I fired the punishing and perfectionist Higher Power that I was given as a child and defined a new one that better fit my current needs. However, since I didn't have a close, personal relationship with Him yet, there was some work I had to do in order to develop trust.

Here's one of the most surprising and exciting ways I did that. I discovered a technique used by monks centuries ago called autowriting. I call it dialoguing with my Higher Power. Autowriting changed my Higher Power from an old man with a long, gray beard, sitting on a throne somewhere far away up in "Heaven" to a close confidant. Those of you who are skeptics will probably roll your eyes and say, "Yeah, right. This is about as credible as a Ouija board or a crystal ball!" Keep an open mind and believe this technique has worked for me and countless others. If you have difficulty at first, keep trying and eventually, you will be amazed before you are halfway through. Remember, "God works in mysterious ways"!

Imagine you're writing a letter to your Higher Power. Write "Dear Higher Power" (or whatever you've named your Higher Power) on the top of a piece of paper. Tell Him all your feelings, fears, everything you might tell a good friend. When you've written all you can, skip a few lines and write "Dear (your name here)". Before going any further, verbally ask your Higher Power to guide your pen. Then begin writing. You will get a comforting, loving response from your Higher Power to your letter! One time, I wrote and asked my Higher Power if He were really answering me or if I was making it up. His response was: "What does it matter, as long as you're getting a loving answer!" (Remember my Want Ad for a Higher Power asked for a sense of humor!)

This exercise helps you find out how much your Higher Power loves you too. I recommend doing this exercise every day for 30 days when you first begin. Mornings are best since you can start your day off in the right frame of mind. Write for three minutes to your Higher Power and then two minutes for your Higher Power's response. (If it takes just five minutes, you have no excuse NOT to do it daily!) Of course, if you want to spend more time, by all means do so.

Consistency is the key to developing this close and personal relationship with your Higher Power. If you don't find relief, I will gladly refund your misery. I wrote a Higher Power letter every day for years, and occasionally still do. It's an excellent form of meditation if it's difficult to sit still and keep our minds quiet!

Exercise 2.3: Up Close and Personal

Dear Higher Power,

Dear (insert your name here),

After a month of writing back and forth between you and your chosen Higher Power, you should have developed a closer relationship and trust that you are being taken care of completely.

Exercise 2.4: The Definition of Sanity

"Okay," you say. "It's fine to believe that there's a Power greater than me, but how can It restore me to sanity? Besides, I don't remember admitting I was insane!"

They say the definition of insanity is doing the same thing over and over and expecting different results. Isn't that what you've been doing? Haven't you been trying to fit that square peg into that round hole hoping that this time it will fit? If you still don't believe you're insane, take one look at how unmanageable your life is around looking for a relationship, or think about how insane you **feel**, and you'll have the answer. Then review *Exercise 1.2: So You Think You're Not a Control Freak?* where you described how your life had become unmanageable. That's insanity at its best, (or worst?) don't you think?

Since you've defined your insane behavior in *Exercise 1.2*, *Exercise 2.4* asks you to describe what **sanity** would look and feel like in relation to the specific problem you identified in the beginning.

Here's what my idea of sanity looked like.

Example: *Exercise 2.4: The Definition of Sanity*

> **Sanity would mean I'd focus on the present rather than project into the future. I wouldn't obsess on getting married and I'd stop judging every man as a potential mate. I'd be happy with what I have right now and stop feeling like there's still one thing missing in my life that could make me happy. I would feel at peace.**

Exercise 2.4: The Definition of Sanity

Write a description of what sanity would look like for you in relation to your specific problem:

_____

_____

_____

_____

_____

_____

_____

_____

Exercise 2.5: Trying to Restore Myself to Sanity

Exercise 2.5 lets you see even more ways you have been trying to control your process. I developed this exercise because I could see I was trying to restore **myself** to sanity by controlling my feelings and behavior. Some of the actions I took weren't necessarily wrong in and of themselves. However, my <u>**motive**</u> was important. I had to examine whether or not I was trying to get things to go my way or really working to develop my spiritual growth. I even found myself using the Steps to try to manipulate God into giving me what I wanted, sort of like making a list for Santa Claus!

Example: *Exercise 2.5: Trying to Restore Myself to Sanity*

Here are some examples of ways I tried to restore myself to sanity before I finally admitted I was truly powerless over this problem and needed a Higher Power's help to restore me to sanity:

1. I read one self-help book a week on codependency;

2. I stayed home instead of going out looking for a relationship;

3. I misused the Steps by trying to have God remove all of the character defects I thought were keeping me from having a man love me;

4. I helped others, thinking my Higher Power would reward me with a relationship.

As you can see, this list contains some behaviors that you might consider healthy for "working on myself." However, my motives were to control God's plan for my having a relationship. That's where I went wrong.

List the ways you have tried to restore **yourself** to sanity so you can examine your motives:

Exercise 2.5: Restoring Myself to Sanity

_____

_____

_____

_____

_____

Exercise 2.6: It's A Miracle!

Being restored to sanity also meant I needed new solutions. That's sanity. Before we move to Step Three, get down on your knees and ask your Higher Power for a miracle. Simply defined, a miracle is a new way of perceiving this problem, a new solution. Also write down any additional solutions that present themselves to you:

Exercise 2.6: It's A Miracle!

_____

_____

_____

_____

_____

STEP THREE: MADE A DECISION TO TURN OUR WILL AND OUR LIVES OVER TO THE CARE OF GOD AS WE UNDERSTOOD HIM

"Our whole trouble had been the misuse of willpower. We had tried to bombard our problems with it instead of attempting to bring it into agreement with God's intention for us." (Page 40, Twelve Steps and Twelve Traditions of Alcoholics Anonymous)

Step Two says we came to believe that a Power greater than ourselves **COULD** restore us to sanity. Not **WILL** restore us. Why does it say, "COULD," instead of WOULD? I think it's because my Higher Power wanted me to ask for help. That's what Step Three is about: deciding that this Power greater than ourselves, <u>COULD</u> restore us to sanity, and <u>WOULD</u> if asked. This Step "calls in the troops (Higher Power)" to do for us what we've not been able to do for ourselves. Here we make the decision to **<u>let things happen rather than make them happen.</u>**

Try these exercises to see how that works:

Exercise 3.1: I'm Too Afraid to Let Go!

Before we can turn a problem over, it's helpful to examine the fears we have about letting it go. In *Exercise 3.1*, you see why you've been so intent on trying to control your problem, and why letting a Higher Power find a solution may terrify you. I've listed my fears about letting go of wanting a relationship below:

Example: ***<u>Exercise 3.1: I'm Too Afraid to Let Go!</u>***

I don't want to give this problem to my Higher Power because I'm afraid that:

1. I won't ever have a relationship or get married;
2. God wants me to Him/Her/Itself, and I have to be alone to be spiritual;
3. God wants me to be with some nerd;
4. I'm supposed to learn how to be happy without a man;
5. I'm incapable of having a relationship because I was never shown how to do it;
6. I don't know how to love.

Looking at this list, it's no wonder I was trying to control finding a relationship and unwilling to turn it over to God! I thought if I let God handle it, I wouldn't get what I wanted! It was clear at that point I needed a new Higher Power because I didn't trust, or even like the One I had. I was afraid my Higher Power wanted me all to Himself, wanted me to sacrifice everything in order to live a spiritual life without a man. I thought He was just teasing me and testing me with men, never intending to let me find a loving husband.

When I recognized this belief I had about my current Higher Power, I went back to *Exercise 2.2*, fired my Higher Power and hired another new One. My fears and my unwillingness to let go indicated the level of my faith in my Higher Power -- **none** in the area of getting a relationship!

You've seen the fears that I had about letting go of solving my problem. In *Exercise 3.1*, make a list of the fears you have about letting go of your problem:

Exercise 3.1: I'm Too Afraid to Let Go!

I don't want to give this problem to my Higher Power because I'm too afraid that:

_____

_____

_____

_____

_____

_____

_____

Your list should show where your faith in your Higher Power is lacking, too. In that case, pray for more faith and make sure you're doing your morning God dialogues.

Step Three tells us even though we might be afraid to turn our problem over to a Higher Power, we can do it anyway. All we have to do is make a **decision**. You don't have to feel like it, or have the faith that God will take care of it for you. Just do it.

Think of it like this: imagine that you are going skydiving. The first time you go, you will probably be terrified. Perhaps you'll be afraid your parachute won't open, you'll crash into a tree, you'll break your leg in the fall, or your cord will break. If you decide not to jump out of the plane because of your fear, you'll never know if your parachute would have opened or not. You never would have enjoyed the exciting sensation of free falling through the air, floating above the earth, seeing the landscape from that height.

However, if you do jump out of the plane, and your parachute does open, and you don't break a leg or get hurt in the fall, the next time you jump, you probably won't be as scared. You'll have had a positive experience of walking through your fears and succeeding, even when you were afraid to jump.

It's the same thing with Step Three. You have to just jump out of the plane -- make a **decision** to turn this problem over to your Higher Power. If you don't jump, or turn your problem over, you might never have the positive experience your Higher Power has waiting for you. If you do jump, you'll have more trust the next time because you will have seen, in hindsight, that your Higher Power's plan for you was better than the one you had for yourself.

Exercise 3.2: I Give Up!

I needed to do more than just turn my <u>problem</u> over to my Higher Power. I had to also turn over everything else: my obsessive thinking, my attempts to force solutions, my thoughts, my actions, my plans and schemes, my ideas about what was good for me, etc. *Exercise 3.2* asks you to make a list of all the things you agree to give to your Higher Power and to **keep your hands off!** Here's an example of some of the things I turned over:

Example: ***Exercise 3.2: I Give Up!***

I AGREE TO TURN OVER TO MY HIGHER POWER:

    1. Fantasizing/obsessing about having a relationship;

    2. The timing of when or if I get married;

    3. Reading self-help books about relationships;

    4. Asking friends to set me up on blind dates;

    5. Giving compliments to men to get them interested in me;

    6. Tendency to flirt;

    7. Focusing on the future;

    8. My judgment of men.

It's your turn now. List all the things you make a decision to give over to your Higher Power:

Exercise 3.2: I Give Up!

I AGREE TO TURN OVER TO MY HIGHER POWER:

    1.

    2.

    3.

    4.

    5.

You've made some important decisions about turning over ways you have been trying to force solutions. Be diligent about monitoring your thinking to make sure you don't take any of these things back now that you've turned them over to your Higher Power. You might want to write them on a slip of paper and put them in a box labeled "For My Higher Power." This will reinforce the thought they are now in your Higher Power's hands, not yours.

Exercise 3.3: Let Go and Let My Higher Power

Once I made the decision to turn this issue over to a Power greater than myself, I found it helpful to reinforce it by physically doing this next exercise:

1. Stretch your arms out straight. Clench your fists tightly. Imagine you are holding onto all the ways you've been obsessing on your problem, along with your worries and the solutions you've been trying to force;

2. Explain aloud to your Higher Power the details of how you've been obsessing on your problem. Continue to hold your fists tightly! Remember, you've been holding onto this obsession for quite a while!

3. Open your fists and visualize letting go of your obsession, as well as the ways you've been trying to control solutions. Tell your Higher Power that you're giving everything to Him;

4. Turn your palms upwards toward the sky. Ask your Higher Power to fill up the empty space inside you where your problem used to be with His Love instead;

5. Close your fists and envision your Higher Power's Love enveloping you and filling you up.

Doesn't that feel great? It should feel like a huge weight has been lifted off your shoulders. If it doesn't, you're probably still holding on, thinking you can't trust your Higher Power to solve this problem in the way <u>YOU</u> want it solved. You're probably still afraid to let go, fearing you won't get the result you ultimately want.

You may need to try a few more of your own solutions before you can finally admit ***complete*** defeat. This is what I call "pre-surrender." Harry M. Thiebout, a friend of AA in its infancy days, called it submission. He said that submission was thinking you would have to give up something you wanted now because you had tried everything and couldn't get the results you wanted, but that you hadn't really surrendered because you still believed that someday, you'd figure out a way to force a solution in order to get the results you wanted. If this is the case with you, you will need to go back to Step One and really examine whether or not you have admitted you're completely powerless over your problem.

Exercise 3.4: <u>My Higher Power's Care, Not Mine:</u>

We are very good at taking care of other people, juggling jobs and home lives, marriage and kids. Step Three is where we can kick back and rest. This Step tells us that our obsession, our desire to solve this problem, as well as our entire life, is in **our Higher Power's** care, not **our** care. That's how I spell R-E-L-I-E-F!! When I completed this exercise, I felt freer than I'd felt in years; free to really be the woman I was without trying to impress anyone else.

Exercise 3.4: My Higher Power's Care, Not Mine:

Describe the relief you would feel if you gave this problem over to the care of your Higher Power instead of continuing to try to solve it yourself. Write your feelings about having it be in His care rather than **your** care.

_____

_____

_____

_____

_____

_____

STEP FOUR: MADE A SEARCHING AND FEARLESS MORAL INVENTORY OF OURSELVES

"Our desires for sex, for material and emotional security, and for an important place in society often tyrannize us...unreasonable fear that our instincts will not be satisfied drives us to covet the possessions of others, to lust for sex and power, to become angry when our instinctive demands are threatened, to be envious when the ambitions of others seem to be realized while ours are not." (Pages 42 and 49, <u>Twelve Steps and Twelve Traditions</u> of Alcoholics Anonymous)

A Fourth Step allows us to investigate why we've been caught in the cycle of repeating the same actions. I found patterns of behavior in relationships repeated themselves. Once I wrote them down and identified the part I played in that dance (like dating the same Nightmare in Shining Armor with a different name and a different face!), I was able to see a hurt, little girl underneath. I didn't realize I was re-living old experiences. As I discovered in completing the Step, relationships bring a whole new set of problems and uncomfortable situations that I tried to avoid. Relationships of all types are Petri dishes for spiritual lessons. Being in a relationship is like pouring Miracle-Gro on our character defects so we can move forward and let go of the behaviors and choices of the past.

Holding onto our past dooms us to repeat it. This Step gives us the chance to identify those patterns we have been repeating which keep us from moving forward. It was those old experiences and beliefs that kept me from having a healthy relationship. That's why one of the most important elements of Step Four is defining "our part". "Our part" is the mistakes **we** made in the problem with people or things we resent.

Please overlook the fact that I've chosen to explain "our part" in terms of the Seven Deadly "Sins" from the Bible: pride, anger, greed, gluttony, lust, envy and sloth. (An acronym is PAGGLES, if you want to remember them). They just happen to be a nice, concise way of identifying the character defects explained in this chapter. Those of you who may be freaking out because I mentioned a specific religious book, I ask you again to keep an open mind. You'll soon see that these aren't like any old idea of the Seven Deadly "Sins"!

For many of us, the word "sin" brings up guilt, shame, bad memories and old concepts. Thankfully, these ideas are based on roles we no longer have to accept. Below, you will see an updated and revised version of these "sins". Notice I put the word "sins" in quotations every time it appears, to remind you, although we're using the same word, we're defining it in a new way.

For women, the "sin" or "our part" can sometimes be subtler than the ways described in the *Twelve Steps and Twelve Traditions*, which was written from a man's point of view. Here are a few examples of what I mean:

- *Pride:* Part of my new definition of the "sin" of pride means "an incorrect relationship with our Higher Power". For example when a woman defines her self-esteem by what a man thinks of her (Ever done that? Not me! Yeah, right!), that's pride. She has made that man her higher power instead of developing a close relationship with her real Higher Power;

- *Pride:* Taking the blame for situations that aren't our fault just to keep the peace (also pride because we are trying to control a situation);

- *Anger:* Because many of us were raised to believe it wasn't "lady like" to get angry, we may not recognize getting angry doesn't have to mean screaming, yelling and violence. I've listed subtle and deadly ways to express anger in the section below;

- *Lust:* Although we might not really crave sex, which is how one usually thinks of lust, we may crave more than our share of love, affection and attention;

- *Envy:* How about when we are not happy with what we have and want to "keep up with the Jones'"? What about when we go to the gym and see "aerobic bunnies" and wish we could be them? Or when we judge someone's insides by their outsides? (I've never done that!) That's the "sin" of envy in a subtle version;

- *Greed:* We usually think of greed as involving money. However, I am often more greedy about giving my time or affection than I am about giving money. I seem to have unrealistic expectations about money, property, prestige and romance from people and from God. That's greed, too;

- *Sloth:* Let's not forget the "sin" of sloth. Because I have often been a workaholic, I thought I never exhibited sloth. However, after doing Step Four, I realized I'm even waiting for a man to create happiness fun in my life and I don't take care of myself in this area. I am too lazy to take care of my own needs and expect someone else to do it for me.

Take a look at the NEW explanations of the Seven Deadly "Sins", updated and written from a women's perspective. I admit I have done every one of these "sins" at one time or another. That's why I know how to define them! However, just to give you another viewpoint, I begin with the Webster's dictionary definition of the Seven Deadly "sin" written in italics:

THE NEW SEVEN DEADLY "SINS"

- **PRIDE:** *Conceit; justifiable self-respect; haughty behavior; ostentatious behavior.*

Pride is simply **not having a right relationship to God.** A right relationship to your Higher Power is when we realize that our Higher Power is in charge of everything, including our lives and we're not. It's also recognizing that we are neither better than nor less than anyone else, because we are all the same in His eyes. We are being prideful when we are trying to control anything, because we are playing God. Some specific examples of pride are:

- Not trusting your Higher Power's process/timing/actions;

- False pride: self-pity, depression, low self-esteem; thinking you're not as good as someone else;

- Thinking you are responsible for taking care of someone else (you're **their** Higher Power); you're in any way responsible for how he or she feels or acts;

- Not saying how you feel because you're afraid you'll hurt someone's feelings, or you'll lose them completely (control)!

- Thinking someone or something else is responsible for your happiness;

- Projecting what you think will happen in the future;

- Making someone else your higher power (giving someone else too much power);

- Being a victim (not trusting your Higher Power to take care of you);

- Taking something personally (thinking it's all about you).

- **ANGER:** *A strong feeling of displeasure.*

Most of us know what anger is. For me, it shows up immediately when someone cuts me off on the freeway. Anger can be tricky though, particularly if you were not allowed to get angry as a child. We can develop more subtle ways to express it. Here are a few you might relate to:

Impatience	Blaming others and ourselves
Criticism	Gossip
Pouting	Withholding love/affection as punishment
Having unrealistic expectations	Depression (anger turned inward)
Judgment	Being demanding
Throwing things, slamming doors (not all that subtle!)	The silent treatment (my personal favorite!)

- **GREED:** *Acquisitive; a selfish desire beyond reason*.

In simple terms, greed can be defined in two ways: 1) not being satisfied with what you have and **wanting more** of it; or 2) not being willing to share what you have. When we get a reasonable share of romance, passion or attention and still demand more, we are being greedy. When we don't want to give up our time or money to help others, we are being greedy.

Here's an example: when I spent 10 hours a day, as well as weekends, working for a corporation, I was being greedy, because I was denying David my time and attention in order to impress my boss and get ahead. (I didn't end up impressing my boss, getting ahead, or even making more money, so greed doesn't pay!)

- **GLUTTONY:** *Eating to excess*.

We can be gluttonous about more than just eating. Whereas greed is wanting more than your share, gluttony is **taking** more than your share of anything: more romance, more passion, more attention, or more intimacy. For example, when I was in college, I dated three men, all of whom thought I was dating them exclusively. (And that was a difficult trick to pull off!) I was definitely taking more than my share, not because I was dating three men, but because they each thought I was dating them exclusively. Another example is my wanting all the men in the world to find me sexier than other women and my working out at the gym for fifteen hours per week to achieve that objective.

- **LUST:** *An intense longing; sexual desire*.

We can be lustful, without having it be directly associated with wanting sex. When attention, affection and romance from a man become an **intense** longing, or a craving, and it occupies much of our thoughts, it becomes an obsession and is the "sin" of lust.

- **ENVY:** *Discontent at the sight of other's excellence or advantages*.

You've heard the expression, "comparing our insides to someone else's outsides." Have you ever wished you had everything a celebrity has, but not considered what their lives away from the cameras are? This is an example of the "sin" of envy. While greed is not being satisfied with what you have, envy takes it one step further by wanting what someone else has. That might mean a good body, a relationship, money or a better life.

- **SLOTH:** *Laziness*.

No one likes to think of him/herself as lazy. But there are lots of subtle ways of being slothful. We might even be workaholics and still be slothful. Here are some ways to think about:

- Wanting someone else to take care of you;

- Wanting someone else to love you without doing the work to love yourself;

- Not helping someone else because it's inconvenient;

- Not having a discussion with someone about your feelings because you're afraid he/she will get angry, will leave, won't love you.

Although in Step Four, you'll identify the part you play in your problem, a word of caution: be especially careful about defining whether or not you're really at fault. I tended to take responsibility for faults that weren't mine, just to keep the peace in a relationship. I learned that apologizing over and over is a polite form of lying, and a way to try to control someone's feelings and actions. Bottom line, when you are doing **Exercise 4.1**, examine closely when you are truly at fault, and when you're apologizing to control the outcome of the relationship.

Here's an example. Several years ago, I had a female friend who loved to point out my mistakes and flaws. In order to maintain the friendship, I would apologize and say that I would try to change and do better. I'd knuckle down and try to fix whatever it was about me that she had criticized, but the result was always more criticism. After about a year of trying to be who she wanted me to be, I used this exercise to take a good look at myself. Thanks to this self-analysis, I stopped apologizing and decided that wasn't what I wanted in a friendship anyway. I finally ended the relationship and took back my self-esteem instead of giving her power over it.

Another example is a long-distance relationship I had in the mid 1980's. (We'll call him Mr. Bicycle Man. He was so into bicycling that he rode 25 miles to work every day, rain, sleet or snow even though he lived in Connecticut. At the time, I wasn't really into working out, and I definitely wasn't into riding a bicycle. But just to impress him, and to try to make the relationship work, I bought a bicycle (which cost more than an average bike - about $800 at the time - since I had to get a smaller frame being only 5' tall!). I began to ride fifteen miles a day. After several months, he was still criticizing the size of my thighs and telling me that if I rode farther and more often, I'd look better. Thankfully, I came to my senses and decided I looked fine, even though I wasn't up to his standards. I ended the relationship after about a year. (God doesn't waste any experiences because I wrote the lyrics for a blues song about that relationship entitled, "There's Lightnin' in These Thunder Thighs". It was recorded by Sapphire, The Uppity Blues Women on Alligator Records!)

Exercise 4.1: Making a List and Checking It Twice

Now that I've defined the "sins" and how subtle they can be, it's time to apply the definitions to our current problem of wanting a relationship. In *Exercise 4.1*, there are five columns. I found it easiest to complete the first two columns and then move across to the others. You will find an explanation of each column below:

- *Column 1:* Whom I Resent;

- *Column 2:* What For;

- *Column 3:* What I'm Afraid of;

- *Column 4:* My Character "Defense" (One of the Seven Deadly "Sins");

- *Column 5:* Behavior I Did to Act Out the Character "Defense".

Here is an explanation of each column:

- *Whom I Resent (Column 1):* resentment is a feeling of anger, frustration, dislike or being uncomfortable with people, places, or things. In French, the word "resentment" comes from the verb "resentir" which means "to feel again". Therefore, resentment is a feeling that you may have right now, but is probably associated with some deeper anger from the past, and you are "feeling it again." That's why *Exercise 4.1* is so powerful. It helps you identify all the people, places, institutions, groups and things you resent now and see their connection to your past. You may have more than one resentment for each person, place, group or institution. Make sure you list them all. Some of us have a hard time identifying our anger, as I mentioned before. The first time I did this exercise, I thought I had nothing to write because I wasn't angry with anyone. So I listed those people I was frustrated with and was afraid of. Don't forget-- you can also resent yourself, your family and your Higher Power!

- *What For? (Column 2):* In this column list <u>why</u> you resent each person, place or thing. If you have multiple resentments against a person, place or thing, be certain to explain the reason why for every resentment;

- *What I'm Afraid of (Column 3):* Behind every resentment, or anger, is fear. That's why *Exercise 4.1* asks you to dig deep and find out what the fear is behind each resentment. There will probably be multiple fears for each resentment. Try to be as thorough as possible in identifying them;

- *Character "Defense" (One of the Seven Deadly "Sins")(Column 4):* This is "my part." Choose which of the Seven Deadly "Sins" you committed as a character "defense" for each resentment (Refer to the preceding pages for an explanation of the Seven Deadly "Sins.");

- *Behavior I Did to Act Out the Character "Defense" (Column 5):* For each Seven Deadly "Sin" that you listed in Column 4 (the Character "Defense"), write the explanation of what behavior you did to act out that character "defense".

Here's my example of *Exercise 4.1: Making a List and Checking It Twice*:

WHOM I RESENT	WHAT FOR?	WHAT I'M AFRAID OF	CHARACTER "DEFENSE" (ONE OF THE DEADLY "SINS")	BEHAVIOR I DID TO ACT OUT MY CHARACTER "DEFENSE"
Jim	Not calling me	◆ He doesn't like me ◆ I'm not worth loving	Pride	◆ Low self-esteem ◆ Made Jim my Higher Power
	Not dating me	◆ No man will want me	Pride	◆ Blamed God for punishing me
		◆ I'm not attractive	Lust	◆ Flirted with Tom in front of Jim so Jim would get jealous and want me ◆ Found out where he'd be and go there just to see him
	Ignoring me at a meeting	◆ I did something wrong to make him angry	Pride	◆ Took his behavior personally and thought it was about me
		◆ I'm not lovable	Anger	◆ I ignored him when I ran into him to get back at him ◆ Cut someone off in traffic after the meeting
God	Not having a relationship	◆ I'll never get married	Pride	◆ Not accepting things are perfect just as they are ◆ Predicting the future
			Greed	◆ Not being happy with what I have
Religion	Making me feel guilty about sex	◆ I'll always feel guilty ◆ I'm a bad girl	Pride	◆ Judging myself; low self-esteem
Myself	Being obsessed with wanting a man	◆ I'll never feel sane	Pride	◆ Made a man my Higher Power

Exercise 4.1: *Making a List and Checking It Twice:*

O.K. Let's see what you come up with now. Write down the people, places, organizations, institutions and things you resent, that frustrate you, or that you are afraid of regarding your problem:

WHOM I RESENT	WHAT FOR?	WHAT I'M AFRAID OF	CHARACTER "DEFENSE" (ONE OF THE DEADLY "SINS")	BEHAVIOR I DID TO ACT OUT MY CHARACTER "DEFENSE"

Exercise 4.2: Here's the Good Part!

An inventory also needs to include taking stock of your good qualities. I found this much harder than identifying the things I do wrong. List the good qualities, as well as all the people, places and things you have in your life for which you are grateful. For example, here's my list:

1. I keep working the Steps no matter what;

2. I am willing to take suggestions even if I don't agree with them;

3. I turn to my Higher Power to help me, even though I think He's not giving me what I want;

4. I live in a fabulous house;

5. I have lots of great friends;

6. I have David.

Exercise 4.2: Here's the Good Part!

_____

_____

_____

_____

_____

_____

_____

_____

STEP FIVE: ADMITTED TO GOD, TO OURSELVES AND TO ANOTHER HUMAN BEING THE EXACT NATURE OF OUR WRONGS

"This vital Step was also the means by which we began to get the feeling that we could be forgiven, no matter what we had thought or done." (Page 57-58, Twelve Steps and Twelve Traditions of Alcoholics Anonymous)

When I first began this journey, I was too ashamed to tell anyone my wrongs. I tried to skip Step Five, and just do Step Four and move on to Step Six without involving anyone else in helping to solve my problem. I didn't see the relevance of sharing that information with someone else since it was just for my own awareness. However, several months later when my behavior hadn't changed and I was still obsessed with finding "the One", I realized I couldn't skip this vital Step. we may drink again. Only after reading my Fourth Step aloud did things begin to change for me.

In reading my Fourth Step to another person, I found that someone could love me unconditionally, even after hearing my faults. I learned to trust someone enough to tell her those embarrassing, subtle actions I was doing to manipulate getting a relationship. Surprisingly, I also found that I was more ashamed of those subtle character defects than I was of the more overt ones.

In *Exercise 4.1*, we identified our wrongs and saw how subtle they could be. These were the Seven Deadly "Sins" we listed in Column 4 entitled Character "Defenses." We also wrote the explanation of our "part" in Column 5. I consider this explanation listed in Column 5 to be the "exact nature of our wrongs," because it explains what we did to act out our "sin".

For example, let's say you identified you were prideful by resenting every woman at the gym who had a great body. The "exact nature" of the wrong is the action or behavior you took as a result of that "sin". These actions or behaviors might be the "exact nature" of that particular "sin" (pride):

1. You decided a body is a measure of someone's worth;

2. You believed you were not as good as someone else because she had a "better" body;

3. You began to work out 3 hours a day to get the same body;

4. You didn't consider what might be going on with that women on the inside.

Step Five's gifts include learning to trust another person, seeing our Higher Power work for us through others and the importance of forgiving ourselves and others.

Now it's time to share your wrongs and the exact nature of them with someone you trust.

Exercise 5.1: The Emperor's New Clothes

In the story, " The Emperor's New Clothes", the Emperor buys a "new suit of clothes" from a salesman who flatters him by telling him it looks so wonderful on him that all of his subjects will respect and adore him when he wears it. Fearing his response if they tell him the truth, his courtiers won't tell the Emperor that his "new suit of clothes" is really his birthday suit! The Emperor is so pleased with his "new suit", that he decides to wear it in an upcoming parade. As the Emperor struts down the street naked, a little boy in his innocence shouts out the truth, that he has no clothes on, and the Emperor realizes he's been robbed and has been made a fool.

Our experience is similar to the Emperor's. Like the sleazy salesman, our fears convince us that acting out our character defects, (or our character defenses as I like to call them) will solve our problem for us. We have been parading around wearing our "new suit of clothes", not realizing these "sins" have actually robbed us of the joy and peace we could have had. We need someone like the little boy before whom we can stand naked, (figuratively, not literally!), admit our faults, who will accept the spiritual truth about us: that we are the wonderful person our Higher Power sees. That's what *Exercise 5.1* is for.

Exercise 5.1 is simple. Find someone whom you trust, (a friend, therapist, minister) and read him or her your *Exercises 4.1* and *4.2*. That way, you can reveal your secrets and hear the spiritual truth. It is important that you do this, because "we're only as sick as our secrets" and the Steps don't work unless you work them completely, as I found out the hard way.

We will always be relieved of the shame and guilt we carry when we share our past mistakes with another person.

Exercise 5.2: Turning the Tables

There is another role involved in working Step Five: listening to someone else's inventory. This is one of the most magical experiences I've been privileged to share with other women. Since there are few books that contain suggestions on how to hear a Fourth Step, here are a few things I've found helpful when I'm on the receiving end of one:

- Eliminate all distractions: no phones, kids, boyfriends, husbands, etc.;

- Start with the Serenity Prayer;

- Explain what the process is and how you'll be doing it. Many women have never done this before and are scared to death so tell her what to expect;

- Listen carefully; don't interrupt;

- Keep a copy of this workbook handy so you can refer to the Seven Deadly "Sins" for each character "defense" to make sure she's identifying it correctly;

- Listen for any "sins" she may have forgotten to include;

- Write down on a pad any comments or questions to review at the end;

- Give your notes to her after you have reviewed them with her;

- Let her know she may feel tired or anxious for a day or so and that's perfectly normal. She's just processing all the feelings she has shared;

- Tell her how proud of her you are and that you are honored that she allowed you to hear some of the most intimate details of her past;

- End the session with a prayer;

- **ALWAYS** tell her that she has done a fabulous and thorough job.

STEP SIX: WERE ENTIRELY READY TO HAVE GOD REMOVE ALL THESE DEFECTS OF CHARACTER

"It is suggested that we ought to become entirely willing to aim toward perfection." (Page 69, Twelve Steps and Twelve Traditions of Alcoholics Anonymous)

In the Twelve Steps and Twelve Traditions book, it says that this Step "separates the men from the boys." In addition to the obvious translation of the Step that separates the "girls from the women", I prefer to think of Step Six as the one that heals our imaginary separation from our Higher Power. This Step is where we becoming **willing** to:

1. Let go of our character "defenses" of trying to control the solutions we identified in Step Four as our "sins";

2. Let our Higher Power show us a new way of living.

Those actions, thoughts and behaviors we identified in *Exercise 4.1* as our character "defenses," are identified in Step Six of the book *Twelve Steps and Twelve Traditions* as "character defects." However, from my perspective, "character defects" are merely behaviors that we adopted in childhood to help us survive and to protect us from painful feelings and/or experiences. For this reason, I call them "character defenses." These "character defenses" may have benefited us in childhood, however, at some point in our adult life, they stop being helpful and started becoming hurtful.

When we get to the point where we are entirely ready to have these "character defenses" removed it's because they have become more of a burden than a benefit. Before we can become willing to let them go, it is helpful to look at what benefits we've been getting out of these "character defenses". That will give us some clues as to why we continue to hold onto them. In my case, once I did this portion of Step Six, I clearly understood why I continued to date one nightmare in shining armor after another. As you'll see from my example of *Exercise 6.1*, I got plenty of benefits from continuing to practice my "character defenses". No wonder I hung onto them for so long!

In Step Six, we examine why we continue to repeat actions, thoughts and behaviors that are now causing us to be so uncomfortable and what benefits we get from continuing to practice them. That way, we can see what we are really afraid of losing if we let them go. Finally, we ask ourselves if we're truly ready to give them up.

In *Exercise 6.1* we'll examine the benefits from hanging onto your character defects (defenses) you identified in *Exercise 4.1*.

Exercise 6.1: Feelin' Bad Feels Oh So Good!

Make sure you have your *Exercise 4.1* in front of you. You will need it to complete this exercise. Here's how it works:

1. In Column 1 of *Exercise 6.1*, write down each character "defense" (defect) that you identified in Column 4 of *Exercise 4.1*;

2. In Column 2 of *Exercise 6.1*, list the behaviors you did to act our your character "defense" as you identified them in Column 5 of *Exercise 4.1*;

3. In Column 3 of *Exercise 6.1*, identify the benefits you've been getting from keeping these character defenses rather than getting rid of them. This might not be easy to figure out, because some of these character "defenses" are so deeply hidden. However, be persistent in your efforts.

Look closely at the example below and you'll see what I mean. I haven't included all of my examples from *Exercise 4.1*, just enough to get you started.

Example: *Exercise 6.1: Feelin' Bad Feels Oh So Good!*

COLUMN 1	COLUMN 2	COLUMN 3
CHARACTER "DEFENSE" (FROM COLUMN 4 - EXERCISE 4.1)	BEHAVIOR I DID TO ACT OUT MY CHARACTER DEFENSE (FROM COLUMN 5, EXERCISE 4.1)	BENEFIT I GET FROM KEEPING THE CHARACTER "DEFENSE"
Pride	◆ Low self-esteem	◆ Can play victim and martyr ◆ Not take responsibility for my choices
	◆ Made a man my Higher Power	◆ I don't have to live my own life and can wait for a man to "rescue" me
	◆ Took Jim's behavior personally	◆ Get to blame someone else
Anger	◆ Cut someone off in traffic	◆ I get to feel in control and powerful ◆ Don't have to feel Jim's rejection and can focus on getting revenge on someone - anyone
	◆ Ignored Jim when I ran into him again	◆ Get to feel self-righteous ◆ Feel like I'm getting my self-esteem back by ignoring him rather than admitting I've made Jim my Higher Power
Greed	◆ Not being happy with what I already have	◆ I don't have to look at my responsibility to create my own happiness
Lust	◆ Flirted with Tom in front of Jim to try to make Jim jealous and want me	◆ I can feel in control and don't have to surrender a relationship to my Higher Power
	◆ Find out where he'll be and go there just to see him	◆ Feel like I'm taking control of the situation

Now here's your chance to find out why you really **_haven't_** wanted to let go of those character defenses!

Exercise 6.1: Feelin' Bad Feels Oh So Good!

COLUMN 1	COLUMN 2	COLUMN 3
CHARACTER "DEFENSE" (FROM COLUMN 4 - *EXERCISE 4.1*)	BEHAVIOR I DID TO ACT OUT MY CHARACTER DEFENSE (FROM COLUMN 5, *EXERCISE 4.1*)	BENEFIT I GET OUT OF KEEPING THE CHARACTER "DEFENSE"

Exercise 6.2: Getting Down to the Core

Exercise 6.1 showed you how these character defenses have been useful to you for all these years. But that doesn't necessarily mean you're entirely ready to have your Higher Power remove them. This next exercise, *Exercise 6.2*, reveals the core beliefs you have underneath the character defenses which stop you from moving forward in your life.

Core beliefs are deeply held ideas we have about ourselves, usually negative ones. They may be decisions we made as a child, often prompted by someone else's input, like our parents or society. These negative core beliefs unconsciously motivate our thoughts and actions. By doing this exercise, I discovered one of my strongest core beliefs was I didn't deserve to live. I recognized I had subconsciously tried to compensate for that core belief throughout my life in a couple of ways. One was by being an overachiever: winning awards, receiving top honors, getting the best jobs, the highest grades, being a perfectionist, etc. Another was thinking if a man loved me, I would then be worthy of living and of being loved.

Some typical core beliefs we may have as women are:

- ◆ We are "damaged goods";
- ◆ We'll only be happy when we have the man, job, money, body, etc.;
- ◆ We aren't worthy of taking up space on the planet;
- ◆ We need to look beautiful and have a great body in order to be loved;
- ◆ The more we "do" or accomplish, the more we'll be loved.

If we don't identify and eliminate these core beliefs, they'll continue to control us and our lives won't change. *Exercise 6.2* helped me do that. *Exercise 6.2* is designed to dig deep under the fears you have if you let go of the benefits you've been getting from keeping those character defenses. It's just one more level in the process to uncover and remove your core beliefs. We'll do this by looking at the fears you have if you let go of the benefits you identified in Column 3 of *Exercise 6.1*. Doing this shows us the close connection between our character "defenses" and the behaviors and beliefs that stem from them.

Exercise 6.2: Getting Down to the Core:

Example: *Exercise 6.2: Getting Down to the Core:*

In Columns 1 and 2, we again list our character "defenses" and the behaviors we did to act them out from *Exercise 4.1*. In Column 3, list the Benefit you get from keeping both the character "defenses" and the behaviors you did to act them out. Here's an example of what my discovery process looked like for Getting Down to the Core. I outlined some of the details to give you an idea:

COLUMN 1 CHARACTER "DEFENSE"	COLUMN 2 BEHAVIOR I DID TO ACT OUT CHARACTER "DEFENSE"	COLUMN 3 BENEFIT (FROM EXERCISE 6.1)	COLUMN 4 MY FEAR IF I LET GO OF THE BENEFIT	COLUMN 5 CORE BELIEF
Pride	◆ Low self-esteem	◆ Can play victim/ martyr ◆ Not take responsibility for my choices	◆ I won't get what I want ◆ It's all my fault	◆ God doesn't want me to be happy ◆ Life is hopeless because I should know the solution and I don't
	◆ Made a man my Higher Power	◆ Don't have to live my life; wait to be rescued	◆ I am all alone and must do life myself	◆ Without a man, I am nothing and life isn't worth living
	◆ Took Jim's behavior personally	◆ Get to blame someone else	◆ It's all my fault	◆ I'm a screw-up and don't deserve a relationship
Anger	◆ Cut someone off in traffic	◆ Feel in control	◆ Nothing is in my control	◆ If I don't control things, I won't get what I want
Greed	◆ Not being happy with what I already have	◆ Don't have to be responsible for my own happiness	◆ I don't know how to make myself happy	◆ I'll never be happy unless I have someone to make me happy
Lust	◆ Flirted with Tom in front of Jim to make Jim jealous	◆ Don't have to surrender to God and can feel in control	◆ I'll never have a relationship	◆ I don't deserve to have one because I'm unlovable

There they are – some of my **core beliefs:**

♦ God doesn't want me to be happy;

♦ I don't know what is causing me to stay single and alone so my life is hopeless;

♦ I don't deserve a relationship because I always mess it up;

♦ I need someone else to make me happy; since I don't have anyone, I'll never be happy;

♦ I am unlovable.

Wow! No wonder I was afraid to let go of my character "defenses" and hung onto them for so long! These core beliefs were underneath them! This exercise gave me compassion for myself as well as patience for God removing them in His time. I could see how they'd protected me from feeling the pain of my core beliefs. They'd served me well as a child. Then, in my childish mind, these core beliefs seemed perfectly logical. However, as an adult, they had now become a liability. If I wanted to have a healthy relationship, and if you want to solve any problem in your life, we've got to let go of those childhood decisions and old core beliefs that motivate our character "defenses".

Time for you to move forward and let go of the old stuff too. That's what the next exercise if for. If you've got your *Exercise 6.1* in front of you, it will be easier.

Exercise 6.2: Getting Down to the Core:

CHARACTER DEFENSE	BENEFIT (FROM EXERCISE 6.1)	MY FEAR IF I LET GO OF THE BENEFIT	CORE BELIEF

Exercise 6.3: Taking the Contrary Action

In *Exercise 4.1* you identified the **behaviors** you have been repeating that hold you back. In *Exercise 6.2* you identified the **beliefs** you have that hold you back. In *Exercise 6.3*, you will design a list of **behaviors and beliefs** that will create a new you for the future. These will be opposite behaviors for those you identified in *Exercise 4.1* and the core beliefs you identified in *Exercise 6.2*. Keeping copies of both those exercises in front of you would be helpful.

In Column 1, list your character "defenses" as you identified them in Column 4 of *Exercise 4.1*

In Column 2, list the behavior(s) you did to act out each defect (found in Column 5 of *Exercise 4.1*).

In Column 3, write down the opposite for each behavior you did to act out your character "defense".

In Column 4, write the core belief you listed in *Exercise 6.2* you need to change.

In Column 5, write an opposite core belief that is positive.

This exercise provides you with new behaviors and new beliefs – essentially, a new life. Take a look at my example. Once again, I have given you just a sampling rather than incorporating every detail from the other exercises.

Example: *Exercise 6.3: Taking the Contrary Action*

COLUMN 1	COLUMN 2	COLUMN 3	COLUMN 4	COLUMN 5
CHARACTER DEFENSE	BEHAVIOR I DID TO ACT IT OUT (FROM *EXERCISE 4.1)*	CORE BELIEF (FROM *EXERCISE 6.2)*	OPPOSITE BEHAVIOR	OPPOSITE CORE BELIEF
Pride	◆ Low self-esteem	◆ God doesn't want me to be happy so I might as well die	◆ Affirm that all of God's children are equally loved in His sight	◆ My Higher Power only wants the best for me so "rejection is His protection"
	◆ Made a man my Higher Power	◆ Without a man, I am nothing and life isn't worth living	◆ Pray and meditate daily to remember God is all I need	◆ I am perfect in God's eyes with or without a man
	◆ Took Jim's behavior personally	◆ I'm a screw-up and don't deserve a relationship	◆ Remember it's not all about me; he might be having a bad day	◆ The results are in God's Hands; I can't screw it up or make it work
Lust	◆ Flirted with Tom in front of Jim so Jim would get jealous and want me	◆ I don't deserve to have a relationship because I'm unlovable	◆ Trust my Higher Power is getting my perfect partner ready for me now	◆ God loves me exactly as I am
Anger	◆ Cut someone off in traffic	◆ If I don't control things, I won't get what I want	◆ Pray before I get behind the wheel	◆ Let go and let God
Greed	◆ Made a man responsible for my happiness	◆ I'll never be happy unless someone else makes me happy	◆ Make a list of things I want and begin to get them without waiting for a man	◆ Happiness is my own responsibility and is based on my relationship with God

O.K. Go for it! Let's try your hand at this.

Exercise 6.3: Taking the Contrary Action

COLUMN 1	COLUMN 2	COLUMN 3	COLUMN 4	COLUMN 5
CHARACTER DEFENSE	BEHAVIOR I DID TO ACT IT OUT (FROM *EXERCISE 4.1*)	CORE BELIEF (FROM *EXERCISE 6.2*)	OPPOSITE BEHAVIOR	OPPOSITE CORE BELIEF

Exercise 6.4: Take It Away, Higher Power!!

Exercise 6.4 forces you to examine whether or not you're really ready to let your Higher Power remove those character "defenses", fears and old core beliefs. Letting go of character "defenses", fears and old core beliefs places the ultimate trust in your Higher Power. Then you will truly be facing life "naked", except for your Higher Power! Your "life" (which we can also define as your actions) and your "will" (which we can also define as your thoughts) would then be in your Higher Power's care instead of yours.

Taking Step Six is a leap of faith. That's why the *Twelve Steps and Twelve Traditions* of Alcoholics Anonymous says Step Six is the one that separates the "men from the boys".

I've only listed two of my character defenses in the example of this exercise since you are merely summarizing information from exercises you've previously completed. However, by listing them this way, you can see all the things you need to ask God to remove when we get to Step Seven.

In Column 1 of *Exercise 6.4*, list the character defenses you have uncovered in *Exercise 4.1*.

In Column 2, list all the

- Resentments
- Fears
- Behaviors
- Benefits from keeping the behavior
- Core Beliefs
- Resentments

In Column 3, write, "Yes" next to each one you are willing to have your Higher Power remove. Write "No" next to each one you are not yet ready to let go and need to hold onto a bit longer.

We're going to ask our Higher Power to remove the whole lot, all at once!

Exercise 6.4: Take It Away, Higher Power!!

"CHARACTER DEFENSES"	RESENTMENTS, BEHAVIORS, BENEFITS, CORE BELIEFS, FEARS I WANT MY HIGHER POWER TO REMOVE	READY TO LET THEM GO?
Pride	**Resentments:** God, myself, Jim, religion	*YES!!*
	Fears: I'll never get married; I'm not attractive; I'm doing something wrong	*YES!!*
	Behaviors: low self-esteem; taking things personally; predicting the future and not staying in today; making a man my Higher Power	*YES!!*
	Benefits from Keeping the Behavior: playing the victim/martyr; not taking responsibility for my life; get to blame someone else; can feel in control; don't have to surrender to God	*YES!!*
	Core Beliefs: God doesn't want me to be happy; I'm nothing without a man; I don't deserve a relationship; if I don't control things, I won't get what I want	*YES!!!!*
Anger	**Resentments:** God, myself, other drivers who don't drive up to my standards	*YES!!*
	Fears: I'll never get married; I'm not lovable; I'm not attractive; I'm doing something wrong	*YES*
	Behaviors: low self-esteem; taking things personally; predicting the future and not staying in today; making a man my Higher Power	*YES!!!*
	Benefits from Keeping the Behavior: playing the victim/martyr; not taking responsibility for my life; get to blame someone else; can feel in control; don't have to surrender to God	*YES!!!!*
	Core Beliefs: God doesn't want me to be happy; I'm nothing without a man; I don't deserve a relationship; if I don't control things, I won't get what I want	*YES!!!!*
	Core belief: Attractive women get attractive men; I don't deserve attractive men because I'm not thin or pretty	*YES!!!!*

Exercise 6.4: Take It Away, Higher Power!!

"CHARACTER DEFENSES"	RESENTMENTS, BEHAVIORS, BENEFITS, CORE BELIEFS, FEARS I WANT MY HIGHER POWER TO REMOVE	READY TO LET THEM GO?

STEP SEVEN: HUMBLY ASKED HIM TO REMOVE OUR SHORTCOMINGS

"But whenever we had to choose between character building and comfort, the character-building was lost in the dust of our chase after what we thought was happiness." (Page 72, Twelve Steps and Twelve Traditions of Alcoholics Anonymous)

Having completed the exercises in Step Six, we have become entirely **willing** to have our Higher Power remove our character "defenses". However, being **willing** to have them removed is entirely different from asking that they be removed. The exercises for this Step are designed to show you how vigilant you'll need to be so you don't return to your old behaviors!

Step 7 can be divided into two parts:

1. Asking our Higher Power to remove the shortcomings,

2. Practicing the opposite behavior, and asking for the shortcoming to be removed whenever you find yourself slipping back to old behavior.

Why the word "shortcoming" in Step 7 instead of "character defect" as it's called in Step 6? There's no way I could know what was in Bill W.'s mind, but I like to speculate that perhaps the word "character defect" is stronger than "shortcoming". Following that theory, the first time you recognize a "character defect (defense)" it's a revelation – a new awakening. However, once you have identified that character defect (defense) and practice it again after you've asked to have it removed, it's just a shortcoming. Of course, since he was such a wordsmith, it could simply be that Bill didn't want to use the same word twice!

In any case, this exercise in Step Seven is designed to ask our Higher Power to remove our shortcomings and our character defenses. I like to do this in a very personal and intimate way, because I want to be sure to have a conversation with my Higher Power to let Him know I'm sincere about being completely done with them. I have discovered a personal letter is the best way to do this. Why not try what works for me?

If you agree, write a letter to your Higher Power in the space below, asking Him to remove everything you identified in *Exercise 6.5* above. Include any additional feelings you have about them, or about having them removed. Just like *Exercise 2.3,* write to your Higher Power as if you were writing to a best friend.

Exercise 7.1: Dear Higher Power

Dear Higher Power,

Dear (insert your name here),

Let's make sure we let these go by doing another exercise just like *Exercise 3.3* by turning them all over to our Higher Power.

Exercise 7.2: Free At Last!

1. Stretch your arms out straight. Clench your fists tightly. Imagine that you are holding onto everything you listed in *Exercise 6.4*: your resentments, fears, character "defenses", your old behaviors, the benefits you get from holding on to them and finally, your core beliefs.

2. List all those things aloud to your Higher Power, while clenching your fists. Imagine you are holding them all in your fists. Remember, you've been holding on to some of them for a long time so hold tightly!

3. Now open your fists and visualize letting go of all of them. Ask your Higher Power to take them from you now.

4. Turn your palms up towards the sky. Ask your Higher Power to fill the space inside of you that you just emptied with His/Her/Its Love instead

5. Close your fists and envision the Light of that Love entering your heart and shining from within.

Exercise 7.3: German Shepherds Nipping At My Heels!

A friend of mine once told me she had been bitten by a German shepherd when she was eight years old, and has been deathly afraid of them ever since. She had recently been struggling with this fear because she and her boyfriend were discussing living together and he had a German shepherd. She would have to learn to live with the dog because they came as a package deal.

The next few exercises helped her get over that fear. However, when she prayed to have this fear removed, she wasn't expecting the response she got from her Higher Power. God put German shepherds in her path everywhere so she could practice getting over her fear! They showed up barking with teeth gnashing in cars parked next to her at the grocery store. Her new next door neighbor moved in with two of them, walking on the street each night when she took her evening stroll. Although she never would have chosen this method of getting over her fear, her fear disappeared became she was so used to encountering German shepherds. She now had a new way of thinking and acting with them.

Since you've asked your Higher Power to remove all the things you agreed to let go of, look out!! Once you've asked for these to be removed, like with my friend, German shepherds will soon be nipping at your heels and will show up all around you. My experience has been, in response to our request to change us, our Higher Power gives us plenty of chances to practice thinking and acting differently so we can let go of those resentments, fears and core beliefs. It is tempting to revert to old behavior when this happens because it's easier than facing your fears or changing that behavior.

As we discovered in some of the previous exercises, we've also believed ideas that aren't true **spiritually** -- ideas such as we're not good enough, we don't deserve love, and we're responsible for making our life work. Our brains, as well as our behaviors, need to be re-programmed, so we can think, as well as act, differently. If your fear or your core belief is still there, that will dictate your behavior, no matter how much you know intellectually it shouldn't.

An effective and powerful way to develop, maintain and reinforce a different way of thinking about those old fears, beliefs and behaviors is to write affirmations. Affirmations re-program your mind to accept a spiritual truth. An example of an affirmation is "All is well in my world." With affirmations, we can reinforce the opposite behavior we identified in *Exercise 6.4* with new thoughts to match. That's why *Exercise 7.3* asks you to write an affirmation for the opposite of each old behavior and core belief. The affirmations are designed to help you face those German shepherds. They're extra insurance that you and your Higher Power will be working together to change your actions **and** your thinking.

Exercise 7.3 asks you to list:

1. The behaviors you did to act out your character defects ("defenses"),

2. The core beliefs;

3. The fears you listed in **Exercise 6.4.**;

4. An affirmation for the opposite of each old behavior and core belief. It's extra insurance that you and God will be working together to change your actions and your thinking.

Here's an example of some affirmations I wrote to help me change my actions and thinking:

Example: _Exercise 7.3: German Shepherds Nipping At My Heels_

OLD BEHAVIORS, FEARS AND CORE BELIEFS	AFFIRMATION
◆ Made Jim my Higher Power	◆ My Higher Power is the One Source of Love
◆ Low self-esteem	◆ I am perfect exactly as I am
◆ Not trusting my Higher Power loves me	◆ I am loved unconditionally
◆ Not accepting things as they are	◆ Everything is perfect in the here and now
◆ Predicting the future	◆ I live in the perfect present moment
◆ Judging my own process	◆ My Higher Power is in charge of my life
◆ I won't ever have a relationship	◆ My Higher Power's plan is in Divine Order
◆ Not being happy with what I have	◆ I am happy, joyous and free
◆ Wanted Jim to ask me out	◆ My Higher Power is my Source of Infinite Love
◆ Went to the meeting just to see Jim	◆ All my needs are met by my Higher Power
◆ I am unlovable	◆ I am perfect exactly as my Higher Power made me
◆ I don't deserve to live	◆ I was created for my Higher Power's purpose
◆ I'm going to be alone forever	◆ I am part of a connected, whole Universe that is loving
◆ Getting angry in traffic	◆ The Universe is in perfect order, despite what I may think or see

Exercise 7.4: German Shepherds Nipping At My Heels

I think you get the idea. Now, go back to your *Exercise 6.4* and write down all the old resentments, behaviors, fears and core beliefs in Column 1 of *Exercise 7.4*. In Column 2, write an affirmation for each fear, behavior and core belief. Copy them down on a separate piece of paper so you carry them with you and say them at least ten times a day.

OLD BEHAVIORS, FEARS AND CORE BELIEFS	AFFIRMATION

Exercise 7.4: Nothin' But the Spiritual Truth!!

In the coming weeks, use these pages to record any situations that occur where you have to practice the opposite behavior to your character defense. Write down whether you remembered to ask God again to remove that shortcoming. Say your affirmation again each time you recognize that you've acted out the character defense again.

Exercise 7.4: Nothin' But the Spiritual Truth!!

SHORTCOMING	SITUATION	ASKED GOD TO REMOVE IT AGAIN?	AFFIRMATION

STEP EIGHT: MADE A LIST OF ALL PERSONS WE HAD HARMED AND BECAME WILLING TO MAKE AMENDS TO THEM ALL

"Since defective relations with other human beings have nearly always been the immediate cause of our woes,...no field of investigation could yield more satisfying and valuable rewards than this one." (Page 80, Twelve Steps and Twelve Traditions of Alcoholics Anonymous)

Exercise 8.1: I'm Sorry, So Sorry

Don't let Step Nine, where you will make amends, stop you from completing this Step. I used to avoid doing Step Eight because I was afraid to face anyone I had harmed. My thoughts jumped ahead to the next Step before I had even gotten there. Remember, this is Step **Eight.**

Step Eight forces us to reflect on whom we have hurt by forcing our self-will trying to get whatever we want in our time frame rather than God's. All we need to do is MAKE A LIST of those persons, organizations, places or things. In order to reinforce that concept, *Exercise 8.1* is divided into three columns:

1. Those to whom you are willing to make amends right now;

2. Those to whom you MIGHT make amends in the future;

3. Those to whom you think you will NEVER make amends.

Recall the people you have hurt with your attempts to force your will getting what you want as it relates to the problem on which you've been working these Steps. Remember to include yourself because we often harm ourselves worse than anyone else.

Exercise 8.1: I'm Sorry, So Sorry

COLUMN 1	COLUMN 2	COLUMN 3
THOSE TO WHOM I AM WILLING TO MAKE AMENDS NOW	THOSE TO WHOM I MIGHT MAKE AMENDS IN THE FUTURE	THOSE TO WHOM I WILL NEVER MAKE AMENDS

Exercise 8.2: How Have I Hurt Thee? Let Me Count the Ways

Once we are willing to make amends to persons, places, institutions or organizations and ourselves, it's helpful to decide beforehand what those amends should be. In order to do that, we need to identify the harm we inflicted on them. Once you've completed this exercise, I highly recommend reading it to a good friend to get feedback, since I know from personal experience that we're not always objective when it comes to making amends. Sometimes, especially as women, we have the tendency to apologize for everything, even for things that aren't our fault. I know I was always ready to say, "I'm sorry", regardless of whether I had really hurt someone or not. If "I'm sorry" stopped an argument, I'd take the blame and apologize, just so someone else wouldn't be angry with me. Then there were times I was completely ignorant of having hurt someone at all.

Here are three different types of amends:

1. Financial amends, where you make financial restitution;

2. Verbal amends, when you apologize for something you did or said;

3. Living amends, where you change your behavior toward a person or organization on an on-going basis without saying anything.

Exercise 8.2 below asks you to list the people, including yourself, places, institutions and organizations you've harmed, to define how you hurt them, and to decide what would be an appropriate amends for each situation. Here's an example of the amends I thought I should make to the persons I had harmed in wanting a relationship:

Example: ***Exercise 8.2: How Have I Hurt Thee? Let Me Count the Ways***

WHOM I'VE HARMED	HOW?	APPROPRIATE AMENDS
◆ Jim	◆ By not accepting his not being attracted to me ◆ By ignoring him at a meeting	◆ Be loving and kind to him (Living amends) ◆ Let him be attracted to whomever he wants to, whether it's me or not (Living amends) ◆ Apologize to him for ignoring him (Verbal amends)
◆ Myself	◆ For chasing after men and giving up my dignity ◆ For making men my higher power ◆ For having so much debt from trying to find "him" ◆ For driving dangerously when I am angry	◆ Stop trying to make things happen; instead, let them happen (Living amends) ◆ Work harder on my relationship with my Higher Power (Living amends) ◆ Pay off my credit cards (Financial amends) ◆ Pray when I am angry and make a phone call to talk about it (Living amends)
◆ Religion	◆ Blaming religion for my being an atheist ◆ Blaming religion for my guilt re: sex	◆ Stop bad-mouthing religion (Living amends) ◆ Make a donation to a church (Financial amends)

I think you understand how this exercise works. Why don't you give it a try now?

Exercise 8.2: How Have I Hurt Thee? Let Me Count the Ways

WHOM I'VE HARMED	HOW?	APPROPRIATE AMENDS

STEP NINE: MADE DIRECT AMENDS WHEREVER POSSIBLE, EXCEPT WHEN TO DO SO WOULD INJURE THEM OR OTHERS

"For the readiness to take full consequences of our past acts, and to take responsibility for the well-being of others at the same time, is the very spirit of Step Nine." (Page 87, Twelve Steps and Twelve Traditions of Alcoholics Anonymous)

Exercise 9.1: Here's the Carrot!

Obviously, Step Nine is where we make our amends to those people, places and things we listed in *Exercise 8.1*. However, before we even begin working on Step Nine, let's take a look at some wonderful gifts we are promised. I call these the "carrots" that our Higher Power puts in front of us to encourage us to make our amends. Page 83 of the Big Book of Alcoholics Anonymous states the promises come true halfway through Step Nine. Halfway through Step Nine, these promises come true in a **new** way each time we do these Steps. Here is what the Big Book says, though I've taken the liberty to number them:

1. *"If we are painstaking about this phase of our development, we will be amazed before we are halfway through.*
2. *We are going to know a new freedom and a new happiness.*
3. *We will not regret the past nor wish to shut the door on it.*
4. *We will comprehend the word serenity and we will know peace.*
5. *No matter how far down the scale we have gone, we will see how our experience can benefit others.*
6. *That feeling of uselessness and self-pity will disappear.*
7. *We will lose interest in selfish things and gain interest in our fellows.*
8. *Self-seeking will slip away.*
9. *Our whole attitude and outlook upon life will change.*
10. *Fear of people and of economic insecurity will leave us.*
11. *We will intuitively know how to handle situations which used to baffle us.*
12. *We will suddenly realize that God is doing for us what we could not do for ourselves."*

In this exercise, write down how you might envision these promises coming true for you regarding the problem on which you're working these exercises right now. Read what I gained out of the painful experiences:

Example: ***Exercise 9.1: Here's the Carrot!***

PROMISE	WHAT IT WOULD LOOK LIKE FOR ME
If we are painstaking about this phase of our development, we will be amazed before we are halfway through	I will be amazed because my obsession with having a relationship and getting married will be completely gone. I will have peace of mind
We are going to know a new freedom and a new happiness	I will be free from looking at every man and wondering if he's going to be my next relationship
We will not regret the past nor wish to shut the door on it	I won't regret all the experiences I've had. I will see how much I have learned from the men I've dated, the mistakes I've made and the lessons I've walked through
We will comprehend the word serenity and we will know peace	I'll be at peace without a man and serene most of the time when I'm alone
No matter how far down the scale we have gone, we will see how our experience can benefit others	I will be thankful for my experiences and my pain because they led me to write this workbook which is helping others with their problems

See how easy that is? That's enough out of me; now you try:

Exercise 9.1: Here's the Carrot!

PROMISE	WHAT IT WOULD LOOK LIKE FOR ME

Exercise 9.2: Doin' the Right Thing

There's only one way to do Step 9. Just do it! Go on out there, make your amends you listed in *Exercise 8.2* and get yourself some of these promises! Remember to start with those whom you are willing to make amends, and I bet that you'll find the process so rewarding that you'll move right through all three columns of that exercise. Good luck!

STEP TEN: CONTINUED TO TAKE PERSONAL INVENTORY AND WHEN WE WERE WRONG, PROMPTLY ADMITTED IT

"For the wise have always known that no one can make much of his life until self-searching becomes a regular habit, until he is able to admit and accept what he finds, and until he patiently and persistently tries to correct what is wrong." (Page 88, Twelve Steps and Twelve Traditions of Alcoholics Anonymous.

Step Ten is the first of the "maintenance" steps. This means that it is a Step that we must work every day, regardless of what problem we are having in order to maintain the peace we achieved from working the first nine Steps. Therefore, you needn't confine your answers for the exercises in Step Ten exclusively to the problem you identified in the beginning. The same will be true for Steps Eleven and Twelve. These can, and should be worked daily.

Many people consider Step 10 to be the only inventory you should take after your initial inventory in Step Four. However, the way the book *Twelve Steps and Twelve Traditions of Alcoholics Anonymous* explains it, this step only covers the day that you are in, not an extended period of time. In fact, that book states that "*some of us found it useful to do semiannual housecleaning,*" (explaining Step Four) as opposed to a daily balance sheet of credits and debits for the day (Step Ten). Therefore, when I work Step Ten, I only review what happened today.

Exercise 10.1 helps you have a format to review what you did today.

In Column 1, list those things you're grateful for, such as a task you performed well, a gift from God (like a parking place!), or even just a smile from a friend;

In Column 2, list the things you wish you'd done better, like spending more time thinking about your Higher Power throughout the day;

Finally, in Column 3, write down the amends that you owe.

By the way, I usually find my gratitude list about twice as long as my other two columns! Also, please note that, unlike the other exercises in the workbook, these rows do NOT have to read across. In other words, the things you wish you'd done better do not need to correlate with the things in Column 1 you listed for which you are grateful.

Here is an example of a Tenth Step:

Exercise 10.1: Daily Reflection

Example: **_Exercise 10.1: Daily Reflection_**

THINGS TO BE GRATEFUL FOR TODAY	THINGS I WISH I'D DONE BETTER	AMENDS I OWE
◆ Did my morning meditation	◆ Got angry in traffic	◆ To drivers on the road: I need to be courteous
◆ Had dinner with my spiritual advisor	◆ Beat myself up for not having a great body	◆ To myself: accept my body as it is
◆ Thanked God for my dog, friends, the past, and David	◆ Still had expectations John would call and got disappointed when he didn't	◆ Living amends to John and me: don't **have expectations**
◆ Have a great place to live	◆ Didn't call Mary back because I'm angry at her	◆ To Mary: talk to her re: why I'm upset
◆ My health	◆ Spent more time reading spiritual books	◆ To myself: not exercising or reading spiritual books
◆ Sunshine	◆ Called Mom to say hello	◆ Call Mom more often

You can use this exercise every day. Here's your own Tenth Step:

Exercise 10.1: Daily Reflections

THINGS TO BE GRATEFUL FOR TODAY	THINGS I WISH I'D DONE BETTER	AMENDS I OWE

STEP 11: SOUGHT THROUGH PRAYER AND MEDITATION TO IMPROVE OUR CONSCIOUS CONTACT WITH GOD AS WE UNDERSTOOD HIM, PRAYING ONLY FOR THE KNOWLEDGE OF HIS WILL FOR US AND THE POWER TO CARRY THAT OUT

"And let's always remember that meditation is in reality intensely practical. One of its first fruits is emotional balance. With it we can broaden and deepen the channel between ourselves and God as we understand Him." (Page 101, <u>Twelve Steps and Twelve Traditions</u> of Alcoholics Anonymous)

The paradox of Step Eleven is this: it's absolutely necessary to admit powerlessness in Step One to obtain God's power in this Step. With this Step, not only do we get emotional balance, as it states in the quote above from the *<u>Twelve Steps and Twelve Traditions</u> of Alcoholics Anonymous*, but we also get the power to carry out God's will. I've been meditating for over twenty years now, so I'm getting better at it. I find the rewards are immense; I get emotional serenity that usually lasts an entire day.

What exactly is meditation? There are as many ways to meditate as there are people who do it. One thing is certain though: prayer without meditation is a one-way conversation. My definition of meditation is letting my Higher Power talk to me, and prayer is when I talk to my Higher Power.

Many of us have a hard time with Step Eleven because we don't know how to meditate. It is difficult to sit still and quiet down our mind. Someone once told me I when I meditate, I should think of my mind as a television set in the background of a party. It is on, but I shouldn't pay much attention to it. My rule for meditation is that I usually stay in it until I don't want to stop. That usually takes about fifteen to twenty minutes. Until that time, I merely accept the fact that my mind is going to focus on my "To Do" list, whatever I think I **should** be doing instead of meditating. I just gently keep bringing my attention back to getting a conscious contact with God.

What does it feel like when you finally get that "conscious contact"? For me, it's like a click inside me, and I suddenly realize there is a loving Higher Power doing everything for me. I also have the sense there is no separation between the rest of the universe and me; everything is connected without borders.

I started out doing Step Eleven by writing "Higher Power Dialogues," where I'd write a letter to my Higher Power, and let him write back, as you did in *Exercise 2.3*. This method was the first that helped me have a personal relationship with Something greater than myself. Prior to doing this, my relationship with God had been at arms-length, to say the least. It was religion, not relationship. It consisted of merely memorizing rules, rites and rituals. My Higher Power was punishing and definitely NOT unconditionally loving. Step Eleven, along with the other Steps, helped me develop and maintain a personal relationship with a Higher Power that has only grown closer.

Exercise 11.1 is the same as *Exercise 2.3*. It is an exercise you can do even if you find it difficult to sit still and meditate, or if you think you have no time in the morning for Step Eleven. You only need seven minutes each day to write a "Higher Power Dialogue." As you did in *Exercise 2.3*, spend about four minutes writing a letter to your Higher Power, telling Him your feelings and your fears about the day ahead. Then take three minutes to let your Higher Power write back to you. Start with "Dear _____" (fill in your name here), as if your Higher Power were addressing a letter to you. Then put your pen to the paper, ask Him to guide your words, and begin writing whatever comes out. Here's an example of one of my dialogues:

Exercise 11.1: Desperately Seeking My Higher Power

Example: ***Exercise 11.1: Desperately Seeking My Higher Power***

Dear Higher Power,

I have a meeting this morning with my boss and I am afraid because I have a tendency to make him my false Higher Power. He scares me because I'm always afraid I'm not good enough and he's going to fire me even though I know deep down inside that's just my head talking. I really need Your help today. Can You please give me the words to say and the power to carry out Your will? Would You please be with me in this meeting and let me know I'm not alone?

Also, I am afraid that I'll never get married. Would You please remove that fear from me again because it cropped its ugly head up yesterday?

Dear Cynthia,

(Here's where my Higher Power gives me the answer)

You know that you have nothing to worry about because you will always and have always had My love to sustain you. Your boss is just trying to do his job and it will help you in the meeting to see things from his perspective. Know that I will never leave you and I am with you always. As for your worry about getting married, give yourself a break. You've spent a lot of years worrying about it and it won't go away overnight. Have faith in Me though that I will remove it when you are ready. Besides, your only job is to show up and breathe and stay in today! I love you!

Exercise 11.1: Desperately Seeking My Higher Power

You can use separate paper for this exercise, since you ought to do it every day anyway. Happy meditating!

STEP TWELVE: HAVING HAD A SPIRITUAL AWAKENING AS THE RESULT OF THESE STEPS, WE TRIED TO CARRY THIS MESSAGE TO ALCOHOLICS AND TO PRACTICE THESE PRINCIPLES IN ALL OUR AFFAIRS

"It became clear that if we ever were to feel emotionally secure among grown-up people, we would have to put our lives on a give-and-take basis; we would have to develop the sense of being in partnership or brotherhood with all those around us. We saw that we would need to give constantly of ourselves without demands for repayment." (Page 116, Twelve Steps and Twelve Traditions of Alcoholics Anonymous)

If we do all the Steps, we are guaranteed each and every time we are halfway through Step Nine, the Promises would come true for us. We now receive another guarantee with Step Twelve: whatever our problem, if we use the Steps to solve it, we will have a spiritual awakening each time. For some of us, a spiritual awakening means we become more compassionate and loving to everyone around us. For others, it begins a lifelong pursuit of trying to understand our Higher Power's will for us, and to strive daily to constantly "improve our conscious contact with our Higher Power" in order to be more spiritually connected.

Whatever spiritual awakening you've had by doing these exercises on the problem you identified in the beginning of the workbook, Step Twelve also tells us that we must now be of service to others by "carrying this message" and "practicing these principles in all our affairs." All the exercises in the workbook up to this point have focused on applying the Steps as they relate to the problem you identified in your own life. In order to keep the peace we have obtained by working these Steps, we now need to use Step Twelve as a way of applying them to your relationship to the rest of the world.

Many people think the Twelfth Step is only about carrying the message about their own recovery program. For example, recovering alcoholics help others who decide that they want to stop drinking. Members of Al-Anon give "comfort and aid" to families of alcoholics, so they can find relief from the pain of living with someone whose drinking bothers them. Compulsive overeaters help other compulsive overeaters to abstain from their trigger foods. This work is the very foundation of the Steps and, for decades, has helped millions of people to remove deadly addictions. It is absolutely essential to work with others facing similar problems if you are continue your recovery. It is also a very literal interpretation of the Twelfth Step.

In this workbook, I have chosen to broaden the interpretation of this Step to address any nagging issues we face, including a complete identity crisis: "Who am I and what's my purpose here on earth?" Once I stopped being obsessed with wanting a relationship, I found it had been masking some bigger questions I had about my life. I began to question my job, my choice of career, my relationships in general. I wanted to know what my Higher Power had in mind for my entire life. Having removed the focus I'd used to avoid these questions, I realized my inner voice, along with my dreams, hopes, wants and desires, was my Higher Power's urging me to find and achieve my **mission** in life – the one He created uniquely for me, whether that's being a singer, a writer, a businesswoman or a teacher. Our Higher Power gave each of us unique talents and gifts as a way of carrying out our mission.

In order to help face this new identity crisis, I designed exercises that use the concepts behind the Twelfth Step, with a less literal and expanded interpretation of it. I made the assumption there is a more universal "message" we are to carry. Some people have a career, even more have a job, but few know their **mission.** When we know what our **mission** is, we are truly clear about who we are and for what purpose we're to use our talents, gifts, wants, desires and dreams. When each of us is "carrying" own unique message we are **being** and doing what our Higher Power intended us to do. Then, because we are doing our Higher Power's will, we feel fulfilled and happy.

The more often we work the Steps in our lives, the more we grow and change. Our mission may change right along with us. As you'll see in the examples below, that's what happened to me. Well, right about now, you're probably saying, "But how do I figure out what my mission is?" Patience! That's one of the things the exercises in Step Twelve are designed to help you do.

I've also expanded the interpretation of the second part of the Twelfth Step, "practicing these principles in all our affairs". Instead of interpreting that phrase to just mean you should be loving, kind and tolerant, the exercises in the workbook help you identify your mission of working to make the world a better place: the causes, goals and ideals about which you feel passionate so you can "carry this message" of love. That might mean working with others who want to recover from an addiction, working to end hunger, helping get an official elected whom you support, or volunteer to create world peace. If we view ourselves as part of a global village, these are "all our affairs". Then you are truly being of service in your life every day in everything you do.

Let me give you a few specific examples of my different interpretation of the two parts of Step Twelve:

1. **"Carrying this message":** means using your talents to be what and whom your Higher Power meant you to be;

   I have assisted quite a few actresses, songwriters, producers, directors -- artist types -- to use the exercises in this workbook. I constantly remind them their Higher Power gave them their art and talent. The fact they love to act, sing, direct, etc. is an indication that's their Higher Power's calling. The best way to be of service, or "carry this message", is to use those talents and art to the full potential that their Higher Power intended by giving it to them. I suggest to them they "carry this message" into every audition, relying on their Higher Power by taking risks in their art. I encouraged them to step "out of the box" and try new things, rather than worry about what the casting director or other cast members think of them. I'm sure it's no surprise they give much better performances! There are plenty of instances where they turned down parts which would have paid handsomely, but which went against the grain of their mission and their moral character. The result every time was they got a better part almost immediately. When they concentrated on their art as their mission in life, rather than concentrating on getting that part, or selling that script or song, their careers magically took off like a rocket. They were using their talents rightly. They were "carrying the message".

If an actress isn't getting acting jobs, it's not necessarily that her Higher Power doesn't want her to be an actress. It may be that her <u>motivation</u> for getting those parts is out of alignment. Perhaps she's not carrying the message she's been given to carry: being an artist who acts. She may be in fear of financial security, which inhibits her at auditions. She may want to be an actress so she can be famous and impress her family, or so she feels some self-esteem. None of those reasons involve being of service to her Higher Power or fulfilling her **mission.**

Here's a perfect example: I helped a beautiful woman who was an actress and a model work on Step Twelve using this workbook. She was offered a part as a victim with no self-esteem who was sexually abused by a number of men. As this woman had actually gone through this experience in real life and had worked the Steps on it, she did not want to take the part and relive those memories, despite the fact that it paid quite well. After doing the exercises in the workbook, she had identified her mission as not being a victim in this area and helping other women to do the same. Because of this, she turned down the part. About a week later, she was offered a much better part for more money and more visibility! The Universe had reinforced her mission by responding to it!

2. **"Practice these principles in all our affairs"**: means practicing your mission as a way of contributing to the world and changing the way you practice it as your mission changes;

The first substance on which I used these Steps was food. After several years I stopped using alcohol. At that time, I was forced to look for a new job because the event on which I had worked for four years was over, and I didn't know what I wanted to do. I prayed to my Higher Power to show me how I could be of service, and one day, while riding in my car, I heard the song "We Are the World" for the first time. I started to cry, thinking of all the people starving in Africa, and the irony of my being addicted to food. I realized at that moment, I was supposed to work on the issue of ending hunger.

I volunteered for a few months at a non-profit organization that addressed that issue specifically, and they hired me as their fundraiser and head of operations. I combined my mission in life at that time, (my talents and experience with non-profit fundraising) with a cause about which I felt passionate.

Three years later, my mission of carrying the message changed to empowering women to feel good about themselves and their bodies. I started writing lyrics. I even had one of my songs, "There's Lightnin' in These Thunder Thighs", recorded by a group called Sapphire, The Uppity Blues Women on Alligator Records, a prominent blues label.

A year after that, my mission changed again. I designed, created, and received funding for, a program to reduce drunk driving at sports venues and county fairs nationwide. This became my job for the next ten years!

Step Twelve is only possible after we've done all the other Steps in order. First, we needed to remove the blocks we put in our own path toward understanding God's mission for us and learn how to be of service to God and others. Once we've gotten in touch with our dreams, our talents and our mission, our life becomes like a speeding train, bringing us happiness faster and more abundantly than we could have imagined. We feel fulfilled. So let's get to it!!

Exercise 12.1: No One is an Island

Write down three issues or causes about which you feel passionately where you believe the world needs to be changed for the better. (Ex: the environment, women's rights, ending hunger, etc.) After each cause, write down your feelings about what is wrong with the way things are and why you think they are that way.

1.

2.

3.

Exercise 12.2: A Perfect World Vision

Spend ten minutes meditating on your vision of the perfect world around each of those causes. Then write down what your vision for the perfect world of the future is regarding your three issues or causes.

MY VISION OF A PERFECT WORLD RE: MY CAUSES

Exercise 12.3: Your Higher Power's Calling

Now pick the vision of the cause that you feel the most strongly about, the one you feel needs healing immediately. Write it down here.

_____

This will be the first part of your mission: to use your talents to make a difference with that cause. You can start by volunteering at a local non-profit that works on that issue, or donate money (although that's the easy way out!) or you can investigate job opportunities that exist within the organizations working on this issue. Remember, that feeling that you need to make a difference is your Higher Power calling. Next, we're going to find out what your talents are.

Exercise 12.4: My Talents

Imagine you are in a contest. The winner is the person who comes up with the longest list of things he/she has the most fun doing in one week. Write down all the things you **LOVE** to do and know you are good at doing.

1.

2.

3.

These are some of the talents your Higher Power has blessed you with. The things we love to do are the things that we do best and the ones our Higher Power wants us to concentrate on. We are meant to be happy, joyous and free by doing what we love.

Now you're going to put your passion together with your talents and come up with the mission statement for your life.

Exercise 12.5: Mission Possible!

A mission statement is a clear definition of what you are and what you want to achieve. Most good corporations have a mission statement in order to make sure they stay on track and produce the kind of products and results their Board of Directors and stockholders want. We could think of our Higher Power as our Board of Directors, so we need a mission statement to keep us on track with the kind of life we want to produce. You can change your mission statement at anytime when it no longer fits with who you are and what you want to do with your talents.

Create a mission statement by bringing all the answers from the previous exercises together here. Fill in the blanks to make a mission statement that you can use as your guide in deciding what you need to do next in your life to fulfill your mission. Keep it with you and say it like an affirmation. Then watch how your life begins to move in that direction, just like magic!

MY MISSION IN LIFE IS TO USE MY TALENTS OF _____(LIST ALL OF THEM HERE) IN ORDER TO CHANGE THE WORLD IN THE AREA OF _____(LIST YOUR ISSUE HERE) TO CREATE A WORLD THAT _____(PUT YOUR VISION OF THE FUTURE HERE).

Okay! You have your work cut out for you! How does it feel to know what your vision of the perfect world ought to be, and how you could use your talents to work with your Higher Power to create that? Good! (For about a millisecond). Then your head says "but I can't make **money** doing that!" This is where Step Three comes in again. Our job is just to show up and look alert. Do the footwork: investigate what people, places and organizations there are that are already working on your issue. It's your Higher Power's job is to bring you the opportunities to carry the message, and to pay you handsomely for it!

The hardest part is staying in faith rather than fear. We're so used to staying in the uncomfortable, simply because it's known. But go back to the exercises in Step Three whenever you feel your faith beginning to wane. The effort will be worth it -- I'm living proof!

Exercise 12.6: Scoring Goals and Objectives

For every mission, you need a plan of how to get there. You need goals and objectives that help you clearly define how you intend to carry out your mission. The dictionary defines a goal as "an end one strives to attain." Objectives are specific actions you take to achieve your goal. Here's an example of my mission for my life, and several goals and objectives I wrote in order to carry out my mission:

Example: *Exercise 12.6: Scoring Goals and Objectives*

MY MISSION: To use my writing abilities, my creativity and my business acumen to make the world a more loving place to live.

GOAL #1: To empower people, especially women, to be all they can be.

OBJECTIVES:

1. To write four songs per year about women being wonderful;

2. To become a mentor and coach and give seminars to women on how to go within to find answers to life's questions;

3. To write a book to help women use the Steps to solve problems;

4. To have a job working with women where I make a difference in helping them find their mission in life;

GOAL #2: To take risks and be living proof of my Higher Power's goodness in fulfilling my dreams.

OBJECTIVES:

1. To accept myself exactly as I am;

2. To take singing lessons and record a demo of me singing one of my own songs;

3. To invest in real estate and stocks;

4. To make at least $300,000 per year

When I first wrote these exercises in 1995, my goals and objectives were different than those you see above. I achieved all of them so I had to come up with new ones!! These are the new ones. Some of the objectives I listed before and achieved were: hold an executive management position in a large corporation, to buy a house in the neighborhood of my dreams regardless of the cost, to make over $100,000 in one year, and write 10 songs.

I like to re-do this exercise every year on New Year's Eve, and then take it out and look at it the following New Year's Eve to see how many of the goals and objectives I've accomplished. Having goals and objectives for every area of your life: financial, spiritual, personal growth, career, and of course, your contribution to the world, is helpful to let the Universe know your commitment and desires.

Now that you've had a really good peek into my life, try defining your own goals and objectives in order to fulfill your mission statement that you wrote in *Exercise 12.5:*

MY MISSION:

GOAL:

OBJECTIVES:

   1.

   2.

   3.

   4.

   5.

GOAL #2:

OBJECTIVES:

    1.

    2.

    3.

    4.

    5.

SUMMARY

Now you've completed all Twelve Steps. Your perception of your problem should be completely different than when you began. You're ready to use them in order to change anything in your life, and to change the world! They are magical that way. Life surely is a dance if you take these Steps!!